Handbags

Turning Hope into Happiness

Cathlene Miner
Aisling Owens Nash
Hopefull Handbags

978-1-917728-04-1

All rights reserved. © 2025 Hopefull Handbags

All intellectual property rights including copyright, design right and publishing rights rest with the author. No part of this book may be reproduced or transmitted in any way including any written, electronic, recording, or photocopying without written permission of the authors. This publication is a compilation of personal memoirs from the authors and views expressed are their own. The authors have made every attempt to provide information that is accurate and complete, but this book is not intended as a substitute for professional medical advice. This book is not meant to be used, nor should it be used, to diagnose or treat any medical or psychological condition. All funds raised from the sale of this book go towards the Hopefull Handbags charity. Edited by Aoife Gaffney. Published in Ireland by Orla Kelly Publishing.

Orla Kelly Publishing
27 Kilbrody,
Mount Oval,
Rochestown,
Cork,
Ireland.

Foreword

When I first founded Hopefull Handbags Global NonProfit, I had no idea that a simple act of kindness would spark a movement that would reach across the world.

It started when I was little, I always wondered if my grandmother had a place to reach out to with no judgment, a place that could assist her to safety, health, happiness, and long-term sustainability, would she have reached out? That thought has stayed with me for years. It is one of the driving forces behind Hopefull Handbags Global, a movement that began as a simple gesture to honor my grandmother, Carolyn, and has grown into something far greater than I could have imagined.

Today, Hopefull Handbags Global operates in several countries, providing survivors of domestic abuse and their children with the tools they need to break free from the cycle of abuse and rebuild their lives.

Hopefull Handbags began with a single handbag. My grandmother always carried her handbag with her, no matter where she went. To her, it was a symbol of preparedness, dignity, and self- respect. That image stayed with me, and when I realized how many women leave abusive situations with nothing but the clothes on their backs, I knew that providing handbags filled with essential items could offer more than practical support, it could offer hope and open the much needed conversation. It was a simple gesture, but it has since grown into a global movement that touches countless lives.

Self-perception is the base of all of our programs. We have seen that by having a healthy self-perception, what you think and feel about yourself everything changes. At Hopefull Handbags, we know that looking to the past does not heal. True healing comes from looking to the future, creating new opportunities, and stepping into a life of strength and empowerment. By shifting focus forward, survivors and their children can begin to rewrite their stories and build a future filled with possibility and hope.

At Hopefull Handbags, we see these children. We see the fear, the confusion, and sometimes the shame that they carry. But more importantly, we see their potential. We see their resilience.

And we are committed to helping them, alongside their parent, find a path to healing. Our SHINE and NEW programs reflect this commitment. By incorporating one-on-one mentoring and a healthy self-perception, we guide survivors through the practical steps of rebuilding their lives, from securing employment to creating a sustainable, healthy, happy future.

One of our most meaningful ongoing projects is Carolyn's Haven of Hope Bridge Housing. This initiative was born out of a realization that staying with friends and family and emergency shelters are just the first step and are very temporary. What survivors truly need is a bridge, a safe, supportive environment where they can transition from crisis to stability. This project, and so many others we've launched, would not be possible without the incredible network of supporters who believe in our mission.

Now, we can look back and see all of our successes with survivors and their children. Our mission achieved: safety, health, happiness, and long-term financial stability for our survivors and their children. Each story is a testament to the power of community and the impact of hope in action. We are reminded daily that change is possible, and that brighter futures can be built from even the darkest beginnings.

The stories shared in this book are deeply personal. They are stories of courage, resilience, and transformation. Each one represents a life changed, a journey from darkness to light. As you read them, I hope you will see what I see: the strength of the human spirit and the power of hope to change lives.

I often say that we all carry our own bags through life, some heavier than others. But when we come together, when we offer support and compassion, those burdens become lighter. We see that there is hope and our futures are bright. That's what Hopefull Handbags is all about. It's about reminding survivors that they are never alone. It's about turning hope into action, action into lasting change and happiness. Thank you for joining us on this journey. Together, we can continue to make a difference, one handbag, one story, and one life at a time. Together We Are Stronger.

Cathlene Miner Founder, Hopefull Handbags Global

(scan the QR code to visit the Hopefull Handbags website)

https://www.hopefullhandbags.org/

Table of Contents

Foreword .... **iii**

Kate Beesley **1**
    Turning Pain into Purpose 4

Eva Storm **25**
    Intuition Unveiled: Transforming Chaos into Purpose 27

Aoife Gaffney **50**
    Those four little words 52

Heather Hargrove **65**
    Wellness is what you do; Health is your result™ 67

Alexis O'Sullivan **81**
    Shine Your Light 83

Orla Kelly **98**
    How Parenthood Led Me to Rewrite My Life .. 100

Annette Cashell **112**
    Exercise is optional, movement is essential 114

Brigid Stapleton **129**
    From a dark terrifying moment to a magnificent triumph 131

Ewa Wiko **148**
    Paintings of Power 150

Sophia Norley **162**
    One Foot Over The Cliff 165

Kerrie Havern **180**
    Thriving Not Surviving 182

Suzanne Goldstein **195**
    Breaking Free, My Journey Through Abuse to Resilience 198

Acknowledgements **211**

Resources **214**

Kate Beesley

Kate Beesley, a personal survivor of domestic abuse, is a trauma and domestic abuse specialist, DASH risk assessor, and educator.

This combination of personal experience and professional expertise fuels her belief that when professionals are trauma-informed and take a factual, empathetic approach to risk assessment and investigation, they can not only restore victims' confidence but also reduce fatalities and improve outcomes for women and girls.

She believes the key to breaking this cycle of abuse lies in education. Women and girls need to be empowered with knowledge about coercive control, stalking, violence, and other abuse-related crimes. By understanding what's reportable and how to engage with authorities, victims can begin to reclaim their power and live without fear.

Everyone deserves to live free from the shadow of fear, constantly looking over their shoulder.

She aims to change how professionals approach domestic abuse and empower women and girls to transition from victims to survivors. By arming them with the tools, knowledge, and support she hopes to help them secure a future of freedom for themselves and their families.

- Her professional qualifications
- Certified Trauma Practitioner
- Certified Meditation Teacher
- Certified Clinical Hypnotherapist
- Certified Breath Meditation Teacher
- Accredited Domestic Abuse, Stalking & Harassment Risk Assessor and Educator (trained by Laura Richards)
- Anti-pathology trauma-informed Advocate (certified by Dr. Jessica Taylor, founder of VictimFocus)
- Diploma in Criminal and Forensic Psychology

Her mission is to help you reclaim your life and empower your family to live free of fear. You are far stronger than you realise. If you've survived everything you've faced so far, you have the strength to overcome this too. What you need are the right tools and knowledge to succeed within a system that often feels like it's set up to fail us. Whether you want to empower yourself or gain the qualifications to help others, I'm here to support you every step of the way. Together, we can turn survival into thriving.

(scan the QR code to visit Kate Beesley's website)

https://www.sayno-das.com/links

Turning Pain into Purpose

"From a single seed of hope, healing begins to take root. Like a phoenix rising from the ashes, we transform, thrive, and soar— proof that even in the darkest moments, the light is always within reach." – Kate Beesley

"If this doesn't work, you'll likely have three years to live."

Those are words no mother of a young child ever expects, or wants, to hear. The thought of planning my funeral was devastating enough but leaving my little girl in the care of her abusive, alcoholic father was an unthinkable nightmare.

For years, I had been managing life with Crohn's disease, but an emergency bowel surgery was a challenge I hadn't seen coming. I survived it. What I couldn't have anticipated was the devastating diagnosis just a week after being discharged: a grade 4 tumour, wrapped around the back of my left knee.

Fighting for my life should have been my sole focus. Instead, I found myself under siege, dodging emotional bullets from the one person who should have been my greatest support. The father of my child, the man I once believed might rise to the occasion in a crisis, did the opposite. He abandoned me when I needed him most, leaving me to face cancer, parent solo, and endure relentless abuse, all at the same time.

It was classic perpetrator behaviour: even a life-threatening illness couldn't stop him from directing attention to himself. During 6 weeks of gruelling daily radiotherapy, I worked tirelessly to keep life as normal as possible for my 3-year-old daughter. My mission was to shield her from the chaos, even as I crumbled inside.

We had been living separately for 18 months at this point, ever since he locked me and our then-13-month-old out of the family home. Despite everything, I clung to the naive hope that we could resemble something of a family unit for the sake of our daughter. Even if it meant living separately most of the time to protect her from his volatility, I agreed to stay married. I felt that maintaining the illusion of a family, fractured though it was, would be a better scenario for her.

Looking back, that decision prolonged the suffering for both me and my daughter. I felt I had been left with little choice. He had systematically stripped away my independence. From the moment our daughter was born,

I was prevented from working or running my business. My savings were drained to fund everything we needed for our little girl's arrival.

When my Crohn's flared severely during that period, I was in no position to push back against his proposals. Staying married and playing along with the façade of a happy family seemed like the only viable option at the time.

Christmas that year was one of the darkest days of my life. I felt blackmailed. There was a threat to cut off financial support and withhold gifts for my daughter. On Christmas Eve, he begrudgingly called to "compromise," inviting me to pick up the gifts so we could load them into my car.

Yet despite the abuse I endured while I attended daily treatment alone, I was expected to behave as though all was well.

I sank into a deep, dark hole of depression during this Christmas time. I wanted to be able to share my daughter's excitement but this felt too hard.

I reached out to my dad, only to be met with judgment: "I told you to divorce him, so I don't want to hear about what he's doing now."

That's when reality hit me, I was truly alone.

Questions began racing through my mind:

How am I going to have my surgery?

Who will look after my little girl?

Should I cancel the operation?

Cancelling wasn't an option. Without the surgery to remove the tumour, I wouldn't have much time left. My little girl needed me, and that thought became my anchor. I thought of my mum, who had defied the odds and fought cancer under equally challenging conditions. If she could do it, so could I.

My daughter was my reason to fight, a miracle I had once manifested into my life, even when the odds were against me.

The answer isn't simple for those who question why I stayed and chose to have a child with a man like that. The reasons were countless, many of them deeply rooted in my childhood trauma of abandonment. The justification I held at the time was painfully clear: *It's the drink that makes him this way.*

I clung to that excuse, even as the challenging behaviour crossed every imaginable line. It was a fragile rationale that began to crumble during one of the darkest moments of my life. I lay in a hospital bed, battling cancer and tending to my daughter, who had fallen gravely ill during my radiotherapy treatment. Instead of showing up for our sick child, I was bombarded with further abuse which added to my stress.

I was already fighting to survive, grappling with the question of how I'd make it to my next life-saving treatment if my daughter needed to stay another night in the hospital. Yet he was consumed by his need to punish me, blind to the gravity of what I was enduring.

Predictably, once the chaos of Christmas and New Year's passed, the familiar script returned: remorseful promises to change, pledges to get help, and declarations of love. But it was nothing more than a performance. This wasn't about me, or even our daughter, it was about saving face.

To him, appearances were everything. At work, he clung to his carefully curated "family man" image. What would he say to colleagues asking about his wife? *"Oh, I left my sick wife and abandoned her in the hospital.* No one should fight this battle alone. No one should feel dismissed or disbelieved.

If I had the insight I have today, I wouldn't have made allowances for the abuse I endured. I would have refrained from arguing my point so often because, in hindsight, this only escalated his behavior. It's not about being right—it's about being safe.

I would have prioritized my emotional well-being and resilience because neglecting those most certainly intensified the impact of the abuse on my overall health, ultimately contributing to me falling seriously ill.

I also would have realized that staying in an abusive marriage wasn't what was best for my daughter, even though I told myself that story over and over. Divorce, he felt, would tarnish his reputation.

Ironically, although he frequently threatened me with divorce, it wasn't something he genuinely wanted. He needed the illusion of a family to maintain his facade, and I had reached the point where I felt trapped.

Even as I reached the end of my tether, I had no choice but to play along. My surgery was looming, and I needed his cooperation to make it happen. Trusting him was a bitter necessity.

He must have sensed the shift in me, the slow unravelling of his control. Abusers are often perceptive when they feel their grip loosening, and as they do, they escalate. That's exactly what happened, the hold tightened and I felt more and more trapped.

I found myself running on autopilot, enduring daily radiotherapy sessions while simultaneously navigating the relentless and challenging behaviour. The hospital staff noticed that I was struggling and referred me for counselling. They believed the full weight of my reality hadn't hit me yet. They even offered to speak to my daughter, suggesting they could explain what was happening in a way she would understand.

But I refused. "No," I told them firmly. "I'm going to get through this. She doesn't need to know anything other than that Mummy is poorly and getting treatment to make her better."

In my mind, there was no other outcome. I was going to beat this. I *had* to.

Six months into my gruelling recovery from the surgery to remove the tumour, the threats escalated to physical violence. One day while our daughter was at school, he cornered me, raising his fist as though to punch me, before hurling a glass at the wall. It shattered against the wall inches from my head.

Later, when I confronted the behaviour, the response was both chilling and calculated. He approached me with a knife clenched in each hand, his eyes filled with rage. "You think you're the big I am, you think you can take me on, well we will see who's the big I am".

Panicked, I ran toward the front door, hoping to raise attention and escape. As I opened the front door, he quickly threw the knives behind the door, concealing them to avoid detection by anyone who might witness the aftermath.

What followed was a torrent of threats. He vowed to drag out any divorce proceedings for as long as possible, promising to make me suffer financially. He said that his intention "wasn't just to punch me it was to "f*** me up". When I brought up how leaving me destitute would affect our daughter, he was unrepentant. He dismissed her well-being entirely, showing no concern for the damage his actions would cause.

All of the blame and responsibility were projected onto me. My illness, he claimed, was a selfish inconvenience. It had jeopardised his career, forcing him to take on parental responsibilities that he felt were beneath him. He insisted that any suffering our daughter might endure was entirely my fault. His cruelty and lack of remorse were staggering, but they were no longer surprising. This was who he truly was.

Afraid that I might reveal what had just occurred, his demeanour shifted once more in a desperate bid to reclaim control. He fell back into the familiar pattern of feigned remorse, this time layered with threats of self-harm, a calculated act of manipulation that succeeded exactly as he intended, keeping me trapped for another 18 months.

During this time, his underhanded behaviour escalated. He began setting up "insurance policies" against me, preparing for the possibility that I might reach my breaking point and file for divorce. His biggest fear was losing control, particularly over the marital home, a place he cruelly forced me and our daughter out of, leaving us in a constant state of housing insecurity.

One such plan was his suggestion to create a Lasting Power of Attorney (LPA), appointing me as his attorney over financial matters. It was presented as a gesture of protection, saying it would ensure that I could manage our finances and access funds if his mental health deteriorated. He claimed it was for the benefit of me and our daughter, and the reasoning seemed plausible. He claimed the idea came from another patient during his first 10-day inpatient stay, following a personal crisis. Allegedly, this fellow patient had implemented an LPA to safeguard their family, and he wanted to do the same.

At the time, it gave me a sliver of hope. I wanted to believe he cared enough about us to protect us, that maybe he truly wanted to change. In hindsight, it was ironic, considering he frequently threatened to cut off financial support as a means of controlling me. But that's the cruel nature of abuse: you cling to any scrap of hope, ignoring the glaring red flags waving right in front of you.

He set up a joint account for us both on the advice of the bank manager. He claimed he couldn't bear the thought of leaving me without access to funds, a gesture designed to reinforce the illusion of care. Despite this, I was too afraid to do anything with the account that was not explicitly approved. I transferred what he instructed me to, as he insisted that if he relapsed, I'd need to restrict his access to the account.

Naturally, when I managed the finances, he lost his ability to use the threat of cutting off financial support. Instead, he turned to a new tactic, threatening to quit his job entirely, ensuring we would all suffer. Despite my careful, and documented management of the account, he still found ways to siphon money for alcohol, gaslighting me whenever I questioned the tell-tale signs. Inevitably, these confrontations would escalate into rage, and he'd blame me for driving him to drink, forcing me to retrieve alcohol for him just to diffuse the situation.

On one occasion, I refused. Our daughter and I had gone to the marital home for what was supposed to be a family day out. When I arrived, I found an empty bottle beside the sofa. He hadn't even bothered to hide it. When I questioned him, he claimed he was "having a clear out" and had found the bottle. My scepticism must have shown because he exploded in rage. He sat down at his computer and began typing an email of resignation to his boss.

"I'll click send if you challenge me," he said, his voice dripping with menace.

"Don't challenge me. I'm in control, not you."

Then came the accusations. He called me a gold digger, to which I snapped, "If I'm a gold digger, I've chosen poorly, haven't I?"

That comment enraged him further. Sensing the danger, I quickly gathered our daughter and left.

Later that day, I received a welfare call from the police. They said they'd encountered him in the village and they had concerns for my safety. They insisted he provide my number. I assured them I was fine, just exhausted from his behaviour, but they weren't convinced. At 2 a.m., two officers arrived at my door to confirm that myself and my daughter were safe.

"We've been sent to check that you are ok," one of them said.

To this day, I don't know what my ex-partner told them to cause such alarm. But his behaviour escalated sharply after that incident, culminating in the moment that finally broke me.

In the early hours of the morning, after yet another argument, he issued his most chilling threat yet.

"Do as you're told, or what's to come is worse than having cancer."

Desperate to appeal to whatever humanity might be left in him, I pleaded, "Please, whatever you're planning, think about our daughter."

His reply was ice-cold: "I don't care. She's collateral damage to punish you. But you can make it all go away if you just do as I tell you."

Those words were the final straw. I called 999, and the police deemed the situation too serious to ignore. Initially, he was asked to attend a voluntary interview at the station and was strongly advised not to contact me. Predictably, he ignored their warnings, and what began as a voluntary interview escalated into a formal arrest, marking the start of a 17-month investigation.

I knew that if I didn't push forward with divorce proceedings and end the relationship for good, the consequences would be severe. His behaviour made it clear that he felt no remorse, and without accountability, the danger he posed would only grow.

Despite being under formal criminal investigation, my decision to file for divorce triggered the retaliation he had ominously hinted at during his final threat. He launched a campaign of vindictive actions aimed at destabilising me and regaining control.

First, he attempted to have me and our daughter evicted from the rental property, where he was acting as guarantor. Then, he orchestrated a SIM card swap on my number, granting him access to my calls and messages. He filed false allegations of fraud with the Office of the Public Guardian, accusing me of mismanaging finances while I was briefly acting as his attorney under the LPA.

Thankfully, I had meticulously kept records of every transaction during my time as an acting attorney, including text message history that demonstrated he had authorised every payment and withdrawal. His attempt to create a "smoking gun" only backfired, as he had made a critical error: by adding me as a joint account holder, the money in the account legally belonged to both of us. Even if I hadn't followed his instructions which I always had.

At the time, I didn't realise the extent of my rights regarding the joint account. I was still too fearful of defying him. I vividly remember the wrath I faced over something as trivial as spending £2 on an ice cream for our daughter without his explicit approval. That level of control left me too terrified to withdraw or transfer anything beyond what he had explicitly instructed, whether it was for my basic living expenses, something he requested I purchase for him, or items for the marital home or our daughter.

True to his word, he did everything possible to disrupt and prolong the financial proceedings, dragging them out to make life as difficult as he could. He attended the final hearing virtually, having missed all of the others. He conjured up the most absurd excuses to avoid attending the other hearings. These conveniently-timed "emergencies" would land him in the hospital for some fabricated illness, only to have him discharged shortly after.

The most ridiculous of these claims involved an alleged encounter with giant hogweed, a plant he miraculously encountered on a route he had walked since childhood. How convenient that this alleged incident happened the day before a critical hearing. It was hard to ignore the pattern: these hospital trips were likely fuelled by his drinking binges, serving only to sober him up temporarily and avoid accountability.

In between these episodes, he engaged in behaviour I now recognise as stalking. His tactics included relentless texts, calls, emails, and even turning up at my door in the middle of the night. He also attempted to manipulate me through the finances, employing every trick in the book to force my compliance. One of the most troubling attempts was using a third party to lure me to the former marital home under false pretences.

Having experienced first-hand, the danger of falling into one of his traps, I wasn't about to be duped again. The last time he had lured me to the house under false pretences, it had escalated to an unsafe and deeply traumatic situation for me and my daughter. Yet, when these manipulations failed, he turned to his unscrupulous solicitor to attempt to blackmail me into compliance, an equally despicable and desperate move to maintain control.

Despite his repeated attempts, the police disregarded his behaviour despite him being under ongoing investigation for 3 serious offences against me.

Meanwhile, his solicitor carried out his bidding at the hearings, presenting proposals that mirrored his initial threats when he locked me out. Her approach suggested I should walk away with only 12% of the marital assets, a calculation he had meticulously outlined to the last penny, even deducting funds he had given me to cover living expenses after his actions forced us to live separately.

He claimed I *chose* to live apart, wilfully ignoring the abuse and toxic environment that left me with no other option. The reality was different. Living as a single parent, forced to move 3 times in 3 years, scraping by on credit cards, and starting over with little more than a few old plates, our clothes, and my daughter's toys, all while maintaining the illusion of a united front to preserve his image and reputation. This was survival, not choice.

Our living arrangements served him far more than they did me. It allowed him to live as he pleased, without the need to hide his deceitful behaviour from his so-called "nagging wife." He could step into the role of family man when it suited him, maintaining his carefully curated facade, while I was left to raise our daughter alone.

Yet my responsibilities didn't end there. I still had to cater to his needs as his dutiful wife.

At one hearing, the judge directly questioned his solicitor about how he had arrived at his proposed figure. When I explained my calculations, explaining that he even wanted to deduct marital debts he had instructed me to pay off, the judge turned to his solicitor with visible disapproval and said firmly, *"No, Miss B."*

The lowest blow, however, came when he attempted to include my critical illness payment, funds meant to support my recovery from cancer, as part of the marital assets. His solicitor argued on his behalf that this money should be deducted from any financial settlement. The judge's disgust was evident. She turned to the solicitor and said, *"Miss B, you know full well that critical illness payments are for the person affected by the condition and are to support their recovery. They do not form part of the marital assets."*

The solicitor, visibly chastised, lowered her head and replied meekly, *"Yes, ma'am."*

This lack of humanity didn't come as a surprise from him, but I had expected better from a legal professional. At one point, he even refused to give me any of the critical illness payment, suggesting "It was *like I made a bet you'd get sick, and I won."* In his mind, any contribution he made was an act of charity, even though those funds were crucial for transportation to my daily radiotherapy sessions and supporting my 6-month recovery after invasive surgery that left me bedridden for 2 months.

At the final hearing, the judge ruled slightly in my favour, awarding me just over 50% of the marital assets and granting me the majority of the proceeds from the house sale instead of a share of his pension.

Yet even then, he couldn't hide his true self. Until the order was read out, he managed to maintain a veneer of composure, but as soon as the judge announced the decision, his mask slipped. His clear disgust and inability to control himself at that moment revealed the man I had been battling all along.

Perhaps if the judge had witnessed this earlier, the outcome might have been more favourable for me given I had full custody of our daughter. But, by then, I was simply relieved it was over, or as over as it could be with someone like him.

Of course, it wasn't over.

True to form, he continued to create chaos, intentionally delaying the house sale, which caused a buyer to back out.

When the house sale fell through, I had no choice but to communicate directly with him to get things back on track as his solicitor was no longer acting for him. Desperate to speed up the process, I attended the property with a police officer. What I walked into left me speechless.

The house was in appalling condition with broken windows, the air reeked of urine, and the garden an overgrown jungle. But what stunned me even more was his demeanour. Standing there amid the carnage he had created, he greeted me with an unnervingly casual, *"Hi, love, you, okay?"*

I could hardly believe my ears. After everything he had put me through. As far as he was concerned, I had subjected him to 17 months of a criminal investigation, potentially facing prison, yet there was no hostility. Instead, he reverted to his well-worn tactic of fake remorse, complete with crocodile tears.

"I'm so sorry. I can't believe I've put you and our little girl through all this. Let me make it right. We'll sell the house together."

I knew exactly what he was doing. He was trying to draw me back in, to regain control. But the house wasn't in a fit state to go on the market, so I played along just long enough to ensure I could clean up the mess he had created. Unfortunately, he quickly realised I wasn't falling for his act.

When his manipulations failed, he turned to coercion. He pressured me to lie to His Majesty's Revenue & Customs Office about our marital status so he could claim the married man's tax allowance. When I refused and reported the truth, his fury erupted. His behaviour escalated once again, and I had to distance myself for my safety. That's when the threats and blackmail resumed in full force.

This time, he was finally charged and sentenced, not for stalking, as it should have been, but for breaching the non-molestation order. Even then, the consequences were laughable: a £160 fine. Despite the Crown Prosecution Service recommending a criminal restraining order, the judge didn't think it was necessary.

It was another slap in the face, a reminder of the system's repeated failure to recognise the gravity of his actions and the ongoing danger he posed. But I refused to let it break me. Instead, I used it as fuel to keep fighting, for myself, for my daughter, and for every survivor who has been let down by the very systems meant to protect them.

Not long after the final hearing, CPS decided my husband didn't intend harm, dismissing the criminal proceedings as though I pursued them purely for financial gain. To this day, I scratch my head in disbelief at their decision.

Even if his threats weren't meant as finality, they were undoubtedly intended to intimidate and cause distress. While they dismissed a "threat to kill" charge, they admitted another crime occurred, only to drop it subsequently.

How can CPS recognise a crime, minimise its severity, and let a suspect walk free because of a technicality? My life was threatened, and my daughter was traumatised, yet they reduced it to something "lesser." Time lapsing after my initial statement shouldn't excuse accountability, but it did.

Adding to the absurdity, the police failed to speak to my witnesses despite initiating criminal proceedings. Without supporting statements, the evidence was incomplete.

After admitting everything he subjected us to, his words were, "But in the eyes of the law, I've done nothing wrong." This is the message that perpetrators receive when they are not held accountable.

This is why survivors lose faith, why many never report abuse, because the process re-traumatises them, gaslights them, and too often lets perpetrators walk free.

I refused to let that response define my story. Instead, it fuelled my resolve. It drove me to pursue in-depth training in violence against women, girls and children. Combining that with my education in trauma and neuroscience, approaching these issues in a trauma-informed way, is a critical step toward real, lasting change.

Today, I use that knowledge to offer trauma-informed training certifications, empowering professionals with the tools, strategies, and understanding to support victims better. This helps address not only the abuse victims suffer but also the re-traumatisation they face from the system.

For survivors, my mission is to empower them to become their own best advocates. I've developed tailored resources and launched *The Domestic Abuse Breakthrough Show*, a ground-breaking radio show dedicated to education, empowerment, and hope. Airing on UK Health Radio and reaching a global audience of 1.4 million listeners, it is the first show of its kind.

I did secure a police apology after highlighting their failings and being acknowledged by a chief inspector. But apologies don't undo the fact that a dangerous man walks free to potentially re-offend, and the next person may not be so lucky.

No one should face this struggle alone. No one should ever feel ignored or disbelieved.

If I could turn back time, here's what I would do.

I would familiarise myself with a safety exit strategy and begin crafting a plan as soon as things started to escalate after my daughter's birth. Being prepared is essential for leaving safely when the moment arrives.

I would have established a safe word with a trusted friend or neighbour. This could have allowed for discreetly signalling the seriousness of the situation when there had been prior involvement with professionals due to his suicide threats.

I would have refrained from confronting my abuser, even when he was clearly in the wrong. This isn't about giving in but reducing conflict and ensuring your immediate safety.

I would have prioritised my emotional resilience and well-being. This is crucial not only for enhancing communication with professionals but also for supporting your physical health.

And finally, I would have equipped myself with knowledge much sooner.

Looking ahead, my priority is to ensure my daughter never finds herself in a position where she cannot recognise the signs of abuse.

Knowledge is indeed our superpower, and my wish for you is to discover meaning from your past by transforming pain into purpose. This is where genuine healing takes place.

This chapter is dedicated to my daughter.

I want you to know how endlessly proud I am of you.

My mission is to create purpose from our darkest days, supporting other women as they transition from victim to survivor—a legacy I leave for you, my beautiful girl.

My hope is that you never again experience what you regrettably did as a child. Never let anyone dim your light. Keep shining like the bright star you are and always remain unapologetically you.

You gave me strength on my darkest days and continue to inspire me every day to turn our dreams into reality.

Our bond is unbreakable as we journey through this disjointed world together, creating memories to treasure along the way.

Mummy loves you, always and forever.

Eva Storm

Eva Storm is a seasoned energy healer, coach, and trainer with almost two decades of experience in helping people heal their inner child and overcome energetic blocks that hold them back in life.

Her specialty lies in crystal consciousness and crystal energy, which she believes can help people establish a direct line of communication with their souls and tap into their inner wisdom.

Through her teachings, Eva aims to empower people to listen to their intuition and interpret the messages of their souls. By doing so, they can gain clarity about their life's purpose and navigate challenges with greater ease.

(scan the QR code to visit Eva Storm's website)

https://evastorm.love

Intuition Unveiled: Transforming Chaos into Purpose

*"Allow yourself to see what you don't allow
yourself to see."*
— Milton H. Erickson

To the conscious parents,
brave souls who dare to look inward, who open their hearts to
healing and their minds to growth.
You are the ones breaking the chains of generational trauma,
paving the way for children to live their truth, to flourish in
their purpose with ease and joy.

This is for all of you,
The ones who came before,
And the ones creating a brighter path ahead.

A Story for Every Soul

My story is not just mine, it belongs to every soul, every child, and every adult on this planet.

It's about the compass we're all born with: intuition.

Why do we need this compass? Because before we were born, we were pure energy, limitless, loving, and formless. A radiant, sparkling soul. But to take on human form, the vastness of the soul had to compress, placing only a part of itself into our physical body.

That part lives in the heart, forming a bridge between heaven and earth. It's like having a direct line to your soul, a cosmic phone call. But instead of words, you hear feelings. I call this connection intuition.

Imagine if you've forgotten you have this line or lost the number.

Don't worry, I'm here to guide you. I'll help you rediscover this connection and give you the tools to navigate life with clarity and purpose, aligned with your soul's wisdom.

My mission is to show how intuition and inner truth are vital, especially for children. Sadly, these gifts can be dulled by trauma or buried under the weight of traditional education systems.

Remember: the obstacle is the path. Every challenge is an invitation to return to your intuition, your soul, and your truth.

Let's reconnect with the compass within. It's been waiting for you.

A Journey of Intuition and Resilience

I was six years old when my parents decided to move back to Belgium. Before that, I lived in the warm, vibrant embrace of Tanzania, at the foot of Mount Kilimanjaro. Tanzania, with its deep red earth, wild beauty, and cheerful spirit, had stolen my heart.

As I write this, a tear rolls down my cheek, and my throat tightens with emotion. I vividly remember playing in the garden with my dogs and Tortue, our 80cm turtle.

But most of all, I remember the sand, how it slipped through my fingers, stirring something profound within me. For hours, I would sit in silence, letting the sand flow through my hands. In those moments, time became both infinite and absent. The world was still, yet alive with motion. Every sound was crystal clear, even in the quiet. My consciousness opened entirely. I understood my parents' struggles with clarity far beyond my years, and yet, I was still a child, simply playing.

It was during these moments that my squirrel guide appeared. The messages came not as words but as an intuitive knowing, a flow of energy that connected deeply with mine. The lessons arrived telepathically, subtle yet profound.

Years later, at age sixteen, I found drawings in an old iron suitcase: a bird, a deer, a bunny, and a squirrel. These images had hung in my childhood room, and suddenly, everything clicked. My guide had been the squirrel all along. But why a squirrel and not the bird or rabbit?

Curious, I researched the spiritual meaning of the squirrel and found it to be deeply symbolic. The squirrel represents trust, resourcefulness, preparation, and communication. It teaches us to find creative solutions, to see possibilities where others see obstacles, and to prepare not just for survival but for a flourishing future.

I realised the squirrel had been preparing me for my journey, not just my life's mission but for the years ahead when intuition and inner knowing would be overshadowed by noise, stress, and trauma.

There came a time when my inner knowing, my intuition, was overshadowed, buried under the weight of noise, stress, and trauma. This shift began when my parents decided to leave the warmth and vibrancy of Tanzania and return to cold, unfamiliar Belgium.

The transition was more than physical; it marked the start of a period where my connection to my intuition felt distant, obscured by the demands of a world that seemed far removed from the freedom and light I had known.

Yet, the foundation of intuition I had cultivated as a child became my quiet strength. It reminded me that even in the darkest times, the connection to my inner compass was never truly lost. It simply waited patiently for me to return.

Traumatised: A Journey from Freedom to Constraint

After the move, life shifted dramatically. Suddenly, I was required to sit indoors all day, confined to a chair, still and silent. It was a world away from my life in Africa, where I spent my days playing outside, running freely beneath the banana trees, and soaking in the vibrancy of the red earth and open skies.

In Tanzania, my mother would visit the school daily, playing the piano while we sang English and Swahili songs at the top of our lungs. The joy and movement were integral to learning, to life itself. But in Belgium, the school system demanded silence. If you wanted to speak, you had to raise your hand. Sitting still was an unspoken rule. It felt stifling, unnatural, even suffocating.

As I did not understand Dutch well, I began to tune into the energy behind words. I also thought visually, taking everything literally, an approach that often caused misunderstandings. At the time, this way of interpreting the world was my survival mechanism. Today, it is my greatest gift as a coach and healer: the ability to see both the energy around words and the subconscious messages hidden within them.

Yet, back then, it felt like a battle. I retreated into my inner world, communicating telepathically with my guide. This intuitive language was effortless, fluid, fast, and clear. But that world began to slip away as external pressures mounted.

I still remember the day my teacher shouted my name. Her voice jolted me like a thunderclap, my cheeks flushing with embarrassment. I hadn't heard her the first few times, and my mother was called in to address the issue. The teacher thought something was wrong with me. I didn't understand the words they exchanged, but I felt their energy: fear and inadequacy.

My mother decided to have my hearing tested. The diagnosis came back: I didn't hear very well.

From then on, I sat in class with fear lodged in my chest, alert like a robot, hypervigilant for the sound of my name. Yet, despite my efforts, I struggled to hear. My intuition, which was once my anchor, began to fade. The connection to my guide disappeared as I shifted focus to the outer world, with its noise, rules, and unrelenting stress.

Soon after, I began to fall ill. My sinuses were chronically inflamed, and I suffered relentless earaches. One night, the pain was so unbearable that I lay on a scalding hot water bottle, preferring its burn to the agony in my ears.

I had never been sick in Africa. But now I was. Why?

- Was it because the teacher's words planted the belief that I might be deaf?

- Was it the stress and constant noise?
- Or was it the ache of knowing we weren't returning to Africa?
- Maybe it was because I no longer had time to listen to my intuition, my inner truth.
- Or it could be all of these combined.

Why does this Matter?

Words hold immense power. They can uplift or diminish. They can open doors to the soul or close them. Words can bring stress or peace, sickness or healing. With children especially, the impact of words, tone, and body language is profound.

Children under the age of seven absorb everything, literally and without question. At this tender age, they cannot yet discern cause from effect what we say to them shapes not only their self-esteem but also their entire future.

A Cultural Rift

The culture shock I experienced was immense. Between the concrete walls of my new environment, I longed for the red earth, the endless green, and the vast blue skies of Africa.

Each night, I cried myself to sleep, quietly praying, God, will you please take me away from here?

Even in my pain, this longing taught me something profound: the power of inner connection, the resilience of the human spirit, and the critical importance of creating spaces where children can thrive, not just survive.

From those early struggles, I've carried forward a commitment to ensure others find their way back to their own inner compass, their intuition, and their truth.

Confusion: The Stories We Remember

If I were to ask you about your childhood, chances are you'd recall only fragments, disconnected images, a few stories told by others, or memories sparked by photos or videos. Much of what we "remember" is pieced together from sensory impressions or narratives we've heard.

For me, my childhood is largely reconstructed through black-and-white photos and countless safari videos my parents took. These recordings tell me what clothes I wore, what car we drove, and what my sisters looked like. They even remind me of small, quirky details, such as my inflatable rabbit rather than a cuddly toy. Practical for a family on the move: deflate, pack, and go.

But memories aren't always straightforward. Sometimes, they're shaped by stories passed down from our parents. And here's the question: are those stories true? What if your parents remember the same event differently?

How do you make sense of conflicting narratives?

I vividly remember our two German shepherds, Laika and Wolfie. Laika was shy, while Wolfie was playful and outgoing. As a five-year-old, I was fascinated by their contrasting personalities. I longed to play with Laika, but her fear of people always held her back.

One day, Laika disappeared. Somehow, I just knew she had died, that she had been run over by a car. My intuition told me this, though I had no direct memory of this. I even "knew" it had been an army vehicle.

Years later, as a teenager, I asked my mother about it. "Do you remember when Laika was run over by an army car?"

She hesitated and then said, "Yes, I remember. But it wasn't an army vehicle. It was me. The dog was sleeping in the shadow of the car, and I didn't see her. When I started the car, I ran over her. It was awful."

I was in shock. My mother had run over our dog. Not intentionally, of course, but the revelation devastated me. It felt as if I had just begun grieving for Laika, even though so much time had passed.

But the real confusion came from my memory. How had I believed for so long that it was an army vehicle?

I realised later that my five-year-old self had created this narrative. I had seen army vehicles pass by our house often, and they had made a strong impression on me. To my young, undeveloped mind, these vehicles symbolised danger. When my intuition told me Laika had been run over, my brain filled in the gap with what I had seen and associated as a threat: an army vehicle.

As children, under the age of seven, we lack the cognitive ability to process cause and effect or grasp the concept of time. For a child, there is no past, and no future, there is only the now. Experiences are a blend of external sensations and inner perceptions, all happening simultaneously and without distinction between what is real and what is imagined.

As we grow, our conscious mind begins to demand explanations. It wants reasons, logic, and clarity to make sense of events. But the stories we create as children often remain embedded in our subconscious, shaping how we interpret and feel about those memories for years to come.

This experience taught me a profound truth: every memory is a mix of outward observation, inner reality and intuition. And sometimes, what we believe to be true is not the whole story, but the one we needed at the time to make sense of the world around us.

The Mind: Choices That Shape Us

When the mind lacks explanations, it fills in the gaps. A developing brain, limited by its capacity, links external events to the images and feelings of the moment. For children, this often means drawing conclusions that become internalised truths—truths that may have little to do with reality.

When parents withhold information or explanations, a child creates their own story, often through an internal decision that leaves a lasting mark. These decisions can sound like:

- I am not important.
- I am abandoned.
- If I stay invisible, I can't do anything wrong.
- I need to behave a certain way to be accepted.
- I am powerless.
- My future is hopeless.

Every decision, whether empowering or damaging, shapes a child's self-image. This self-image becomes a reflection of their personality and ego, like a mirror. But what if that mirror is foggy, scratched, or shattered into countless pieces?

It can take a lifetime to gather and mend those fragments, a process of mourning and healing that has no clear endpoint. Yet, it's not the event itself that causes trauma. It's the inner choice made in response to that trauma that defines whether the self-image grows stronger or more fragile.

Can a Positive Choice Arise from Trauma?

Absolutely. I was 14 when I was kicked out of class for the umpteenth time. I didn't mind; I did it on purpose. The school system felt stifling, an outdated, uninspiring structure where we learned things disconnected from real life. Teachers seemed disinterested, and I felt invisible in a world that treated me like a child when I already felt like a young adult.

That day, standing frustrated in the corridor, I made a life-changing decision: I will be someone who truly listens to others, especially children and young people. I will ask, "How are you?" because no one asked me.

My rebellion was my survival mechanism, fueled by pain. My father had died a year earlier, and I missed him terribly. He had gone back to Africa to prepare for the family to follow. I was ecstatic at the thought of returning to the continent I loved. But it never happened. He died there, and we never said goodbye. There was no funeral, no closure.

I intuitively knew he had passed because I felt his presence beside my bed the night before. He had come to say goodbye energetically. I have never told this story to anyone. Who would understand? The grief was unbearable, and out of that pain, I made another decision: I would rebel even harder.

What began as frustration became defiance, from unruly to indomitable. It was my armour, my way of navigating a world that didn't see or hear me. On the outside, I appeared adventurous and daring. But at night, I cried myself to sleep, surrounded by the shards of my broken inner mirror.

From Pain to Purpose

Still, that moment in the school corridor imprinted on my soul. It planted the seed of my life's mission: to listen, connect, and help others find their voice.

But life took me on a detour. I became a marketer, built a thriving advertising agency, and let my creativity flow freely. My intuition gave me an edge. I could instantly see the branding vision for a business or person, down to the smallest detail. It was a world dominated by men, and I took pleasure in surprising them. Clients often expected to meet a man. I'd show up looking like a teenager, with two braids and a sharp mind, outsmarting them all.

For 10 years, my business boomed. But then chaos struck. One employee took 6 months' leave for a back injury. My partner, overwhelmed with burnout, could no longer hold a pen. Everything fell apart.

During the chaos, I felt a deep ache in my heart. I knew I couldn't sustain the business alone. And then, as if whispered by the Universe, I remembered the promise I had made as a teenager: I would listen to children and young people.

It was clear. The time had come to honour that promise.

I closed my agency and changed the course of my life. What began as rebellion and pain transformed into a mission rooted in compassion, connection, and listening.

The Power of Inner Choice

Trauma doesn't define us; the choices we make in response to it do. Even in our darkest moments, we can choose growth, purpose, and a stronger sense of self.

The mind may try to explain and rationalise, but the heart knows the truth. And sometimes, it takes chaos to remind us of the promises we made to ourselves long ago.

What Intuition Is—and What It Is Not

To understand intuition, we must first clarify what it is not.

Your intuition is not the constant chatter of your thoughts, the to-do lists, or the inner debates about daily life. That is your conscious mind at work. Nor is it the whirlwind of emotions, desires, or goals tied to your personality and ego.

Intuition is something far deeper. To access it, you must step away from noise and sink into stillness, into the present moment, the now.

Being still is not about effort but release. It is like letting sand slip through your fingers or gazing at a quiet landscape. You can cultivate stillness in solitude, through walks in nature, by the sea, in the mountains, or simply by sitting on your meditation cushion.

In this silence, your intuition finds its gateway, a space to deliver the messages of your soul, the truest essence of who you are. It bypasses the false constructs of the ego and speaks directly to your heart.

The moment your mind leaps to "Oh, I need to send that email," the door to intuition closes. To truly receive your soul's guidance, you must understand a simple truth:

Focus is everything. The mind cannot multitask and remain connected to intuition.

Intuitive insights often arrive when you're fully present, during a shower, while jogging, chanting, or deep in meditation. It is in these moments of surrender, when you are simply being that the magical door to intuition opens wide.

Intuition is your direct connection to your soul, your guide to living authentically and fully. To hear it, cultivate silence. To trust it, embrace stillness. In doing nothing, you receive everything.

What Is Your Soul?

Your soul is vast, far beyond what the mind can fully comprehend. Imagine this: if your physical body were the size of your navel, no more than a centimetre, then your soul would be as large as your entire physical body. This is not a literal measurement but a way to grasp the immense scale of your soul. Children's souls are no smaller than adults'; their physical bodies simply haven't caught up yet.

Though your soul cannot fully reside in your body, it connects with you deeply through your heart.

My daughter, Sarah, a highly intuitive and sensitive child, once voiced something profound: "Why are adults so childish with me? Can they not see I'm the same size?"

Her words perfectly captured an experience I had felt all my life. She wasn't saying her soul was bigger than others, but her access to it was. Her soul, older and wiser, was deeply integrated with her heart. This allowed her intuition to be razor-sharp.

Sarah possesses, what I call, crystal energy, a crystallised consciousness far beyond trauma. This purity enhances her intuitive clarity. The truth is, the more trauma you heal, the more your access to your intuition sharpens.

Her heightened intuition often left me astonished. At just five years old, we left home one day, and Sarah exclaimed, "Mammy, the front door is still open."

I was certain I had locked it and dismissed her concerns. But her insistence grew, her voice rising with urgency until she began crying and stomping her feet. I finally turned back, partly to prove her wrong.

At home, I checked the front door. It was locked. But Sarah, with unwavering certainty, said, "No, Mammy, not that door."

Then it hit me. She meant the door to my shop next to our house. I checked. It was indeed unlocked. The door had been open all night, leaving the art gallery vulnerable. Sarah's intuition had saved me from a potentially devastating loss.

Her gift was undeniable. But this wasn't just about her. It was a mirror for me.

She reflected my traumas, and also my potential and my gifts. She challenged me to grow, to listen more deeply, not only to her but also to my own intuition.

Learning to honour her intuition became a lesson in honouring my own intuition. In doing so, I stepped into a more profound understanding of both of our souls.

Breaking the Cycle: A Journey of Healing

Every week, I dedicated at least 6 hours to meditation, and sometimes, I meditated for 3 days straight. I read countless books to heal myself, determined to break free from the patterns that held me back.

One evening, as I sat reading The Journey by Brandon Bays, my young daughter joined me. Though she couldn't yet read, she calmly said, "It's good you're reading this book now. It will cure your earache and sinusitis."

I was stunned. How could she know? Could she sense the energy of the book or my energy? She just knew intuitively and without explanation.

Trusting her wisdom, I travelled to London to attend Brandon Bays' training, taking her with me. I wanted her to witness the power of healing first-hand and, as her mother, to set an example of self-transformation.

But my deepest motivation was clear: I refused to pass my traumas onto her. The cycle of generational pain had to end with me. No cost was too high, no effort too great. I believed fully in my ability to manifest whatever was necessary to achieve this goal. A broken child was not an option.

After the training, I was healed, just as my daughter Sarah had said.

Today, I incorporate Brandon Bay's The Journey technique into my healing sessions, helping others find the freedom and transformation I experienced. It reminds me of the power of intuition, the importance of listening, and the beauty of breaking free for ourselves and for future generations.

The Art of Kintsugi: Turning Wounds into Gold

Have you heard of the Japanese philosophy of kintsugi? It is the ancient art of repairing broken pottery with gold, making the object even more beautiful than before.

Kintsugi teaches us that just as a broken cup can become a masterpiece, our scars and imperfections can become our greatest strengths. The word itself, kin (gold) and tsugi (connection) reminds us that healing is a process of transformation, where our wounds are not hidden but celebrated.

Your painful past is what makes you unique. Each scar tells a story of resilience, growth, and the alchemy of turning pain into wisdom. Let every crack and flaw remind you of your strength, and carry them proudly with your head held high.

Your healing is your gold. Embrace it.

The Power is You

Imagine, for a moment, how your life would have unfolded if you had stayed in complete, unshakable connection with your intuition. How different would things have been if, as a child, you deeply understood that every solution, every answer you ever needed, was already within you?

Think about it. Wouldn't life have flowed with more ease?

- No unnecessary drama pulling you away from your peace.
- No financial struggles rooted in self-doubt or fear.
- No unresolved relationship issues because you'd always know how to navigate love and connection.

But here's the truth: The purpose of your intuition is not to bypass the challenges and lessons of life. It exists to guide you through them. It's there to remind you that every challenge carries wisdom, and every detour can realign you to your true path if you're willing to listen.

Your intuition is the language of your soul. It speaks in whispers, nudges, and feelings, urging you to move toward the life you were born to live. A life aligned with your unique blueprint, a design tailored to your highest potential.

You didn't come here to live by accident. You came with a purpose, a mission woven into the fabric of your being. And when you listen, when you trust the quiet power within, life unfolds in ways that are both magical and deeply fulfilling.

Ask yourself:
- What is my intuition telling me right now?
- Am I willing to follow its guidance, even if it feels uncertain?

The answers are not outside of you; they've never been. They are within you, waiting for you to discover them. Listen. Trust. Act. The power is, and always has been, you.

Connecting Back to Source: The Power of Intuition

One of my life's purposes is to guide people back to their source, their divine essence, by helping them reconnect with their intuition. I am devoted to weaving intuition into the fabric of our daily lives, bringing it into schools, businesses, and perhaps even your life.

Let me affirm this truth: each time you heal a trauma, you open the door wider for your intuition to flow seamlessly into your consciousness. With each healing, your soul's voice becomes clearer, louder, and more profound. The next step is to listen, trust that inner voice and act upon the wisdom of your soul rather than the limited reasoning of the ego mind.

Because I am deeply in tune with my intuition, I see possibilities where others see roadblocks. I see solutions where others see nothing. This perspective transcends context, it applies to family dynamics, parenting, education, business strategy, and the complexities of life itself.

My second purpose is to empower parents, teachers, and caregivers to guide the new generation with conscious intention and positive influence. This approach is free from manipulation or punishment, focusing instead on a holistic foundation of respect, trust, and shared responsibility.

To hold space for others, we must first embark on our own healing journey. I have guided countless parents, grandparents, and teachers in reconnecting with and healing their inner child. True transformation begins within, when we change ourselves, we pave the way to empower a new, extraordinary generation. A generation deeply attuned to their intuition, effortlessly expressing their inner wisdom and living their true potential.

As an international trainer in intuition, communication, hypnosis, coaching, and healing, I've dedicated my journey to helping others unlock their innate potential. Through my work in remote healing, I have witnessed how reconnecting with intuition and the inner child can transform lives and elevate consciousness.

A Mother's Journey of Understanding and Growth

As a mother, my greatest challenge and gift was raising my daughter, a profoundly intuitive and sensitive soul. Her vibration was incredibly high, and I had to elevate my frequency to fully understand her and guide her through the dense energy of this earthly plane.

She saw the world with a clarity that few could fathom, and this clarity often came with deep emotional pain. When she learned of war, she cried through the night and became physically unwell. "Why would anyone harm their brothers and sisters?" she asked. "Why would you kill children? Or animals, only to place them on a plate?"

I came to understand that children, especially highly intuitive ones, are deeply affected by the surrounding energies. Low, stagnant, or discordant frequencies can make them physically ill, emotionally overwhelmed, and spiritually disconnected.

My goal is to preserve her freedom and light by maintaining my high vibration. In doing so, I could hold space for her gifts to flourish. Yet, I couldn't shield her entirely from the outside world. When she entered school, she encountered systems and individuals who were unable to understand her higher way of thinking. Teachers underestimated her, and the curriculum felt irrelevant to her vast, intuitive intelligence. She faced bullying from peers who didn't understand her gifts.

Our education systems are designed for linear thinking, yet these New Age children, crystal, star, and indigo souls, operate at a multidimensional level. What they need isn't more facts and rules but nurturing, understanding, and the freedom to explore their boundless potential.

Empowering Highly Intuitive and Sensitive Children

This journey inspired me to write my book, *'Guiding a Crystal Child: Empowering their highly intuitive gifts and unlocking their true potential'*.

If you seek to better understand these remarkable children, this guide offers insights and tools to honour their intuitive nature and protect their spiritual gifts.

But let's not forget: every child is, by nature, a highly intuitive child. When we allow them to play freely, to feel joy, and to remain trauma-free, they effortlessly access their intuition. Our task as parents, educators, and caregivers is to create environments that nurture their innate wisdom instead of suppressing it.

A Call to Action

This is not just a personal mission, it is a collective calling. Let us raise our vibrations and meet these children where they are. Let us heal ourselves so we can hold space for them to grow, thrive, and fulfil their purpose.

Together, we can co-create a world where intuition, freedom, and joy are not just possibilities but the foundation of a new way of being. Let's align our souls, work together, and transform this vision into reality.

The time is now. The power is in us.

This chapter is dedicated to my daughter.

Aoife Gaffney

Aoife Gaffney (a closet introvert) is the founder of Prudence Moneypenny Coaching. She is an award-winning international Certified Money Coach, relationship and life coach empowering women to take charge of their lives and earn more money. She is the Regional President of the Professional Speaking Association in Ireland, Institute of Banking and a Qualified Financial Advisor.

She is a certified EFT practitioner, hypnotherapist, NLP master and trauma-informed practitioner. Using her signature light-hearted coaching method, she works with women who are looking to take up, shake up, make up or break up with their relationships with themselves, their partners and/or their own money stories.

When she is not coaching, hiding, drinking coffee, writing books, cleaning or tidying, she works in education, primarily supporting adults with additional needs. She is a proud tree hugger and sits on the volunteer board of Directors of a non-profit, native, Irish tree planting co-op, An Dulra. www.andulra.ie.

She is a keynote speaker, multiple best-selling author and mediocre cook. She loves all things purple, really good coffee and even better wifi. She does not take herself too seriously. She holds a world record for promoting female entrepreneurs online. #laptopworldrecord.

She currently lives in Ireland, in her tiny house, and frequently dreams of warmer climates and a bigger house. She is a regular contributor to Irish newspapers and radio.

(scan the QR code to visit Aoife Gaffney's website)

https://linktr.ee/prumoneypenny

THOSE FOUR LITTLE WORDS

"Everyone has a plan; until they get punched in the face." – Mike Tyson

Possibly the most annoying 4 words to say to someone are "Can you not just……?".
Can you not just leave him/her?
Can you not just stop doing that?
Can you not just leave your job?
Can you not just stand up for yourself or fight back?

These questions often oversimplify the complex realities that some people face, leading them to feel stuck, trapped and powerless.

When we are stuck in the middle of something, the hardest part is seeing the light. It's like being stuck in a traffic jam and trying to see past the cars to the nearest exit. It can appear as though everyone else is in the faster-moving lane. The reality is that this is never the case. Everyone else's problems are always easier to solve than your own.

It is always easier to be objective than subjective. It is always easier to look out rather than in. When we take emotion out of the equation and stick to the facts, answers are often much easier, but decisions are difficult because they involve emotions. We know what we must do, but taking action and doing it can be another story. It's called the "knowing-doing gap".

My life has imploded many times, and will probably continue to do so because that's my life. Everyone has a plan until they get punched in the face. I have been metaphorically punched in the face many times. I'm still here; I'm still standing. My resilience and mental health have been tested and will continue to be tested as I push through my fears.

Several times, I found myself stuck in substantial debt because life punched me in the face. Each time was the result of a relationship breakdown. I had dated a few "good on paper" men. Men who were gorgeous to look at but hell to live with. Men who initially came across as charming and attentive but were deeply insecure and needed to dominate someone else to make themselves feel better. I also lacked the ability to talk about money and held the unique ability to attract the wrong people. I asked myself many times "Can I not just leave?"

At one of my lowest points, I found myself financially and emotionally drained by a manipulative partner. At first, he showered me with attention and kindness, aligning with my love language of acts of service[1]. But soon, the mask slipped. His grand gestures became debts, and his charm turned into control. This is a common pattern with abusers.

I was overjoyed and filled with emotion that someone would shower me with such positive attention. I was treated to wonderful experiences such as meals out, cinema visits and even a cleaner for my house. I lived in a small house and generally didn't mind cleaning, but I was unwell, and this felt like such a luxury.

Before long, I was being asked to contribute financially to these acts of service. There would be an excuse such as delayed incoming payment or an unexpected bill. I would be asked to pay for the experience until he was paid and assured that I would be reimbursed. I never was and the excuses continued. When I tried to address this, I was told I was being calculating and that surely, as a couple, all outgoings should be shared. What was mine was his and what was his was also mine. Sadly, I was left with substantial debt, mostly incurred by him.

I could not see what was under my nose. I could not see that I was being manipulated and used.

---

1 Chapman, G., & Campbell, R. (2016). *The 5 Love Languages/5 Love Languages for Men/5 Love Languages of Teenagers/5 Love Languages of Children*. Moody Publishers.

The subtle control continued. I was being isolated from my friends and family. If I planned to see some friends, there would be a mysterious last-minute emergency, and he would need to borrow my car, or he would ambush me with a surprise dinner. On a few occasions, I stood my ground and went ahead with my plans, but I would inevitably receive a phone call or several asking me to come home as something had happened or he missed me, and I would have to make my excuses and leave.

I was studying for my undergraduate degree at the time. This proved challenging because it required me to spend long hours studying or writing assignments. I set up a study support group, and we would rotate in each other's houses to share childcare and knowledge. If I was studying, I would be interrupted repeatedly with offers of tea, snacks, neck rubs or requests to use the computer for some urgent personal matter. Once, he even needed to borrow the pen I was using. The requests would always be prefixed with "I'm sorry to bother you because I know you are so busy but … you know how much I support you …I love you so much… I can't live without out …" and so on.

He insisted on me being around even though he would disappear for hours at a time and sometimes days, nearly always having borrowed my car. If I tried to discuss this, I was accused of being overly sensitive or paranoid. What need did I have to go anywhere when I was studying so much and my friends could come to me?

My friends could see the manipulative behaviour but I could not because it had crept up on me and slowly became my normal. I began doubting myself, and lost the confidence and ability to make decisions for myself.

The pivotal moment came when I discovered evidence of illegal substances in the glove box of my car. I was looking for the service manual as the car was being repaired. A bag of white powder fell to the ground at my feet like a live grenade. The mechanic and I just looked at it and then at each other, each of us too embarrassed to say anything. I picked it up, put it into my pocket, smiled sweetly through gritted teeth, paid my bill and vowed never to return to that particular garage again.

Suddenly, everything fell into place. I understood why he never seemed to have any available funds. He had a high-paying job with considerable responsibility when we met, but had a disagreement with a superior and chose to leave. He had managed to secure a subsequent role in a similar company but the same thing happened. I had been facilitating an addiction without knowing it. It explained the mood swings, the long absences, the constant need to borrow money, and the heightened anxiety that I was the only one who could resolve.

Why did I stay? All I had to do was leave, but life is never that simple. If it was, there would be no need for coaches, counselors, therapists and mental health specialists. There was a secondary gain for me if I stayed; the need to feel needed. Even though I felt trapped, my self-confidence was so low that unconsciously I felt that being needed was better than being alone. I had deep-rooted emotions of guilt and shame. I was guilted into allowing him to stay and the shame of another failed relationship was overwhelming. I was led to believe that if I left, I would be betraying any promises we had made to each other.

Looking back on this, I see now that promises are agreements that stem from conversations that happen inside relationships and not all promises are honourable. Everything around us that seems fixed, such as matters of law, legally binding contracts, marriages, property etc, are the direct result of agreements. Even money is an agreement. I felt so much shame for trying to re-engage in an agreement stemming from a conversation I was not truly part of.

"Shame must change sides." – Gisele Pelicot

Choosing to remain in an abusive partnership is a daily betrayal and the wounds can become deeply embedded trauma. It is a death of 1,000 cuts. Co-ercisive control is highly dangerous because it is subtle and the victim rarely sees it happening.

The day that a plastic bag of drugs fell on the ground was a turning point, and so was a Christmas gift I received that year where I was gifted a lampshade. It was a very nice lampshade, but not exactly what I would describe as my ideal gift. Ironically, this was more upsetting than the plastic bag. It was an indication of how little I was valued. Because I struggled to value myself, I was allowing other people to undervalue me in return.

Yet I found an inner strength I did not know I had. I remember driving home and rehearsing the speech in my head. I did a few calculations on the back of an envelope and figured out what I owed and how to support myself. It would be easier because there would be one less drain on my meagre resources.

By the time I pulled into the driveway, I had gathered all my strength. I called on every deity I could think of to guide and support me. I put my key in the door, walked in and said the words, "We are over; you need to leave; I will give you time to pack." The look of shock on his face quickly turned to anger and then the manipulation began. I stood my ground and he realised I was serious. The next 24 hours were not the easiest but I made it through. As soon as he left, I changed the locks and arranged with one of his friends to collect his possessions. I was finally free.

I subsequently sold the lampshade.

I now reflect on this time with compassion for myself. Every day I chose to stay, I was affirming that I was not worthy of something better or more. I felt stuck, powerless and trapped. I felt I had nowhere else to go.

"If you are going through hell, keep going."
–Winston Churchill

I have gone through hell so many times that I could nearly guide myself through without Google Maps if the route did not keep changing. But it does, and so do I, which is why I, and so many others, find ourselves repeating patterns of unhealthy and unproductive behaviour.

I have experienced different types of abuse and bullying over the years. In most cases, those negative experiences came from people close to me that I cared about. Those stories no longer belong in writing because I gave myself permission to let go and set healthy boundaries. Boundaries are not about getting others to bend to your will, boundaries are about ourselves and making clear decisions about what we are willing to accept. Letting go is not about forgetting. Our experiences are what shape us. Letting go is about moving on, moving forward and finding a new path.

Unhealthy patterns of behaviour or patterns of behaviour that do not serve us come from many different sources, some of which we may be aware of and some of which can be sneakier. Sneaky behaviours can come from genetic predispositions, childhood traumas that we have pushed into the cupboard, or simply inherited beliefs that we have never questioned.

I could entertain you, the reader, with even more tales of woe and complex traumatic cellular memories; however,

I have made a conscious decision to release myself from all that has held me back so far. I am aware of most of my chaos, my trauma and my patterns of behaviour so far, and I have built a new future for myself by healing my past.

I am aware that I will never be 100% aware of everything, which is life's paradox. There will always be something else to learn, something else to forgive, someone else to forgive, something to push past because when we are striving, we are living, and the more we live, the more we strive to live. In his book, *The Big Leap*, Gay Hendricks talks about upper limits or self-imposed limitations that we often place on our success, happiness, and personal growth.

The older I get, the more comfortable I become with myself and the more aware I am of my upper limits. I use a daily mantra from this book;

"I expand in abundance, success, and love every day, as I inspire those around me to do the same."

Our self-worth is an unconscious price that we expect others to pay. When we raise the bar for ourselves and step into our personal power, we increase our worth, expecting more, receiving more and being more.

A few years ago, I made a commitment to myself that I was no longer willing to accept bad behaviour from other people. I also made a commitment to myself that I would never shed another tear over anyone, particularly men. I would never give anyone power over me again. I gave

myself permission to walk away, whatever walking away needed to look like in that moment.
- I walked away from my keyboard because someone had sent a disrespectful email. Rather than get upset or reply in anger, I gave myself permission to process and reply when I felt calmer.
- I walked away from a bank because the service was poor.
- I walked away from a store because the staff member's attitude was poor.
- I walked away from a conversation mid-sentence because the other person was behaving badly, and I needed to cool off, otherwise risking saying something I might later regret.

Walking away does not mean forever. It does not have to be final. It is simply about being clear about what you are willing to accept.

That decision was liberating. It was not about being disrespectful but about being true to myself and increasing my self-worth. I built a new future by healing my past. I had to feel the pain before I could heal it.

Leaving that relationship marked the beginning of a profound healing journey. I had to confront guilt, shame, and long-standing patterns of people-pleasing. Healing meant setting boundaries, rediscovering my self-worth, and prioritising my mental health.

The more I increased my self-worth, the more I began to respect myself. Using the tools from Maxell Maltz's book, Psycho Cybernetics, I began to work on my self-image. This started with a simple task of wearing make-up every day, even on a day I was not leaving the house. The postman might want to ask me out. I had previously been forbidden to dress up or enhance my appearance in case I attracted unwarranted attention. My "going out" clothes were physically destroyed.

This tiny action led to a shift in my mindset. I felt I was worthy of self-care and investment. I gave myself permission to put myself first. I also began to pay myself first, a practice I continue to this day. Paying myself first does not mean I ignore everything else. It simply means that I am at the top of my list of bills. I add money to my savings account before paying any bills. This sends a powerful message to my subconscious mind that I am worthy.

Releasing debt and the unhealthy relationship that was attached to it allowed me to feel more personally successful. Success is often linked to net worth but true success comes from within.

Do you have a clear vision for your success? What does it look like? Success is fluid and flexible, not hard and rigid. It is a process, not a destination. Success means different things to different people.

To succeed in life, we need three driving forces:
- Something to do
- Something to look forward to
- Someone to share it with

My "something to do" is my life purpose, which has taken me a while to figure out. My life purpose is to gently kick people in the ankles to become the greatest version of themselves and to leave a legacy they are proud of. This is my role as a coach. I coach people around money, personal growth, and how to structure their stories.

My "something to look forward to" frequently changes as I always have something to look forward to. At the time of writing, I am looking forward to the launch of this incredible, life-changing book.

My "someone to share things with" also changes because I am fortunate to have different people with whom I can share different things. The person you share things with can be multiple people and does not have to be a significant other or family member.

Being part of the launch team for this project afforded me the privilege and honour of supporting the authors on this cathartic journey of self-discovery and personal growth. As their coach and writing mentor, I not only heard their stories firsthand but also helped structure their words and figure out how their messages could serve others.

Through our stories, insights and personal experiences, we can begin to heal the wounds of the past and make life easier for those coming up behind us. We can only begin to heal the past by facing it, and what better way to face it than by releasing that pain through the written word? When we speak our truth, we can become powerful.

My advice to my younger self and those coming up behind me;

- Figure out your values and focus on them because they will be your driving force.
- Put yourself first and guard your mental health.
- Release judgment, it will happen regardless but it is up to you to ignore it.
- Focus on what's good in life to attract more of it.
- Do something for someone else.
- Practice daily gratitude and forgiveness. Forgiveness starts with you.
- Surround yourself with people that uplift you.
- Use daily journaling as a cathartic process.

If you encounter someone in a challenging situation, replace judgment with compassion. Use a different set of four little words.

- What do you need?
- How can I help?
- Let me help you.
- Use me for support.
- There is no judgement.

Heather Hargrove

Heather Hargrove, widely known as Heather Healer™, is a #1 international bestselling author, certified trainer, and motivational speaker with over 25 years of experience in health and wellness. Featured on ABC, CBS, and Fox News, Heather inspires others to embrace self-love and personalized wellness for optimal health. She is the visionary behind *Ideal Body Image*, empowering individuals to live their healthiest, happiest lives through her philosophy: "Wellness is what you do, Health is your result™."

(scan the QR code to visit Heather Hargrove's FB Page)

https://web.facebook.com/HeatherHealer/

Wellness is what you do; Health is your result™

We live in a world where health feels elusive, bombarded by conflicting information from countless reports and self-proclaimed experts. We value glitter over simplicity, fast results over persistence, and hope for health from a bottle or the latest "magic" solution. However, wellness and health—while deeply connected—are fundamentally different. To achieve optimal health, your wellness practices must take center stage.

In today's fast-paced, relentless world, convenience dominates. However, this over-reliance on convenience often triggers health issues that could have been prevented.

The environment we live in and even the smallest choices we make profoundly impact our well-being, both now and in the future.

One Step at a Time: Turning Defeat into Victory

What we eat, how we live, and how we nurture ourselves—the sum of our daily choices builds our health.

We live amidst constant noise, quick fixes, miracle promises, and confusing advice. But here's the truth—true health doesn't come from shortcuts. It's built through the actions you take every single day.

"Wellness is what you do; Health is your result™."

This ideology didn't come from textbooks or seminars. It was born through pain, perseverance, and a determination never to give up. It shaped my life and my mission to help others reclaim their health.

What actions are you taking today to prioritize your wellness?

The Brace Years

At fourteen, I was diagnosed with scoliosis, lordosis, and a severe spinal twist. My spine became a complex roadmap of misalignment: an "S" curve winding through my lumbar and thoracic regions with a pronounced twist, a "C" curve in my cervical spine, and lordosis in my lumbar spine, causing it to curve inward excessively. This wasn't just about my posture—doctors warned that without treatment, my ribs could dangerously press against my lungs and heart, possibly puncturing one or both, with potentially fatal consequences.

Surgery was the recommended course of action. But my protective and forward-thinking father chose a less invasive, long-term approach instead. I was fitted for a rigid back brace to prevent further curvature.

Custom-molded from hard plastic, the brace encased my torso, running from hips to chest and secured by thick Velcro straps. It was heavy, restrictive, and unyielding—a constant reminder that I was different. Wearing it for twenty-three hours a day wreaked havoc physically and emotionally. The brace compressed my insides to the point where meals became torturous. I frequently threw up, succumbing to both defeat and isolation.

At the time, I resented not having surgery. Yet, as I reflect now, I am profoundly grateful for my parents' decision. Thanks to that brace, I've experienced a lifetime full of activities I might have otherwise lost.

However, there was one place where the brace couldn't bind me. That place was the water.

Swimming was my only chance to remove the brace, aside from my allotted hour of "freedom" each day. It offered more than just physical relief—it offered respite on many levels.

I can vividly recall *that first day*. Standing in the locker room, fingers trembling slightly, I unfastened the Velcro straps. Each rip felt like a symphony echoing around me. When the last strap came free, I lifted the brace off and felt its absence acutely, my unused muscles quivering. But alongside that weakness came an overwhelming sense of freedom.

I walked to the pool's edge with lighter footsteps and a heart full of anticipation. Beyond, the pool stretched out like a ribbon of turquoise, shimmering with possibilities, alive and welcoming. The sounds of laughter and splashes coming from within brightened my mood even more.

Sliding into the water was not just a release but more like reuniting with an old friend. Its coolness embraced me, whispering, "You belong here." And I did.

The water freed me entirely—muffling the world's noise and allowing me to focus on my strokes. Vulnerability faded. Confidence surged. No longer was I "the girl with a brace." I was capable, confident, and free.

The pool quickly became my sanctuary. Each time I pushed off the wall, I was reminded of the power of small victories. At first, I swam only short stretches, halfway to the wall and then back. Slowly, I built my confidence, trusting the water to carry me. The deep end, with its unseen bottom, felt like a quiet dare: Can you go the distance? Each time I tried, the answer was a resounding yes.

What began as cautious self-exploration evolved into passion. Realizing I had a natural talent for swimming, I joined the competitive swim team. Swim meets, and camaraderie became my refuge. With every lap, I discovered my own resilience.

We practiced before and after school, giving me several precious brace-free hours each day. Competitive swimming became more than just an activity; it was liberation. I was moving forward, finding my rhythm, and embracing the freedom that came with letting go.

Water became my greatest teacher. It taught me to trust myself and my journey. Every stroke was a declaration: I can do this. I will do this.

Two profound lessons were learned during this time:

1. Strength isn't just physical—it's about showing up, even when everything hurts.
2. Freedom isn't a singular moment—it's built through small, consistent steps forward.

These lessons haven't just stayed with me. They continue to empower me.

So, I ask you: What small, consistent step can you take today? What could bring you even a moment of freedom?

The Super Mom Rollercoaster: Pushing Too Hard

When the brace came off, I didn't look back. Marriage, children, career, I wanted it all and was determined to do it all, have it all, and be it all. I pushed my body relentlessly, striving not just to be Super Mom but, in some ways, Super Heather. I threw myself into life, large and in charge, wearing my relentless drive like a badge of honor.

I lived on coffee, burning the candle at both ends and kept long hours trying to juggle everything. I worked odd jobs that fit around my children's schedules. I refused to slow down, believing it was proof of my dedication and capabilities with a "Nothing can stop me," attitude.

Inevitably, something gave. Days lost to exhaustion and pain turned into weeks. My body was sending clear signals, but I refused to listen. Instead, I pushed harder, convinced I could power through. The rollercoaster of overexertion and collapse continued for years, all while my children were still at home.

Each crash taught me a hard truth: that relentless drive without rest leads to breakdown. Yet, I couldn't seem to stop. I viewed rest as a weakness. Slowing down felt like failure. And so, I continued until my body finally gave out, forcing me to confront the consequences of my choices.

Rock Bottom and the Oregon Crisis

Not long after our children had grown, we moved to Oregon. What I thought was the sadness of an empty nest turned out to be more serious. Because I hadn't listened to my body's warnings, I spiralled into adrenal fatigue. This wasn't just burnout. It was rock bottom.

Some days, even lifting my head off the pillow seemed too much, with the weight of exhaustion pressing down on me. The once-simple rhythm of daily life had become an insurmountable challenge.

On weekends, my husband would lovingly lift me into the car, his quiet strength a constant through my haze of exhaustion and drive me to the coast. Sometimes we rode in silence, other times we'd listen to music, but my favorite was when he would sing to me. Those drives became a quiet ritual, an unspoken lifeline. He knew what I needed, even when I didn't have the strength to say it.

The beach greeted us with its steady song and the rhythmic roar of the waves, carrying a promise I couldn't yet grasp. He would steady me as we walked toward the water, his arm an anchor as my feet sank into the cool, forgiving sand. I leaned on him as the salty breeze tingled my skin and filled my lungs. The sea stretched endlessly before me, the frigid waves lapping at my feet, their icy embrace both startling and soothing. The horizon blurred where the water met the sky, an infinite expanse that seemed to echo the parts of myself I thought I had lost.

Once again, I found refuge in the water. Even in my weakest moments, the sea grounded me. It moves with purpose, rhythm, and a strength that feels untamed and reassuring. It taught me that nothing is permanent, but there is beauty in persistence.

With the ocean's unyielding presence and my husband's unwavering care, those moments by the water became a ritual of healing. Together, they reminded me that even in my frailty, I was part of something vast and alive, a force that ebbed and flowed but never stopped moving forward.

The Power of One Step

Then came the darkest day, when even the promise of the seaside couldn't lift the heaviness. I couldn't muster the strength to get out of bed, let alone go to the bathroom.

My body, which had once carried me confidently through life, now felt like a burden I couldn't bear. Every movement seemed insurmountable. In quiet desperation, tears streamed down my face as I whispered into the stillness, "Dear God, if this is as good as it gets, please take me now."

I wasn't suicidal, just spent, empty. But in the silence that followed, something deep within whispered back: "That's not it."

Those three simple words carried the weight of possibility.

I sat up, trembling, and swung my legs over the edge of the bed. Slowly, I dressed in sweats and shoes, shuffled to the front door, and stepped outside, my eyes fixed on the fire hydrant down the block. What had once been a few seconds' walk now seemed like an eternity.

"Here goes nothing," I thought, taking my first shaky step. The air felt sharp in my lungs, and every movement met resistance, but I pressed on. Reaching the hydrant, breathing heavily, I clung to it like my life depended on it. Tears of both pain and pride streamed down my face. Now, if I can get back."

The next day, I went a little farther. Each step became a victory, each breath a testament to resilience. The fire hydrant wasn't just a marker. It became a beacon of renewal. What began as a desperate crawl toward survival transformed into a steady practice of resilience, one small step at a time.

I began to rebuild my outlook on healing and what I wanted my life to look like. Drawing from my early years as a Nutrition Educator, I embraced functional nutrition, focusing on whole foods tailored to my body's needs. I adopted intentional wellness practices into every aspect of my life and redefined moderation, not as a concession to weakness but as a commitment to balance and sustainability. I realized that slowing down wasn't a failure. Moderation wasn't a weakness. True weakness lies in the lack of balance that comes from rejecting moderation.

Each step I took mirrored the ocean's waves: a rise, a fall, and the promise of movement. I came to realize that healing wasn't linear and didn't need to be.

Part of the Reason I Went Full Throttle

Part of the reason I went into manic overdrive was because I failed to truly love myself. I never felt like I was enough, not pretty, slim, strong, or smart enough. I somehow thought that with my busyness and achievements, I could earn that sense of being "enough." But the truth is, I already was enough. I always had been.

Our bodies are walking miracles. Every breath, heartbeat, and step is a testament to our worth, which is evidence of how extraordinary we are, yet learning to love myself fully and unconditionally was one of the hardest and most profound lessons of my journey. Loving who you see in the mirror isn't about vanity. It's about something much deeper, it's a recognition of your worth, your resilience, and the beauty of the person you've become. There's power in embracing your reflection with pride and gratitude.

Who I am, and who you are matters. I am worthy. And so are you.

From personal renewal to professional mission

My journey from personal renewal to professional mission wasn't instantaneous. It was built step by step, just like my healing. It became more than just a transformation; it became my purpose. I saw countless people struggling, worn down, hurting, and stuck in cycles of self-judgment and self-harm, searching desperately for answers. I could see their pain, their silent cries for help, and it mirrored the struggles I had once endured. As I began to reclaim my health, I felt a powerful pull to help others navigate their paths to wellness. I understood firsthand the struggle of feeling stuck, overwhelmed, and lost in the noise of quick-fix solutions. This shared struggle became a bridge—the foundation on which I built a new chapter for myself and others.

I returned to my foundational training as a Nutrition Educator and layered it with new knowledge in holistic wellness practices. I pursued certifications, attended seminars, and immersed myself in the latest research on functional nutrition, stress management, and integrative wellness. Each new piece of knowledge wasn't just a puzzle piece—it was another step forward, another piece of hope. This wasn't just about surviving; it was about living vibrantly.

But I didn't stop there. My work evolved beyond nutrition. I began to recognize how deeply connected our physical, emotional, and mental health truly are. This understanding inspired me to develop programs that addressed wellness from every angle including mind, body, and spirit. I created personalized wellness plans, taught workshops, and spoke at events, sharing not only strategies but also my own story of struggle and resilience.

Every healing opportunity I've embraced stemmed from small, deliberate choices. These weren't grand, cinematic moments but small, brave acts of self-love. Those choices didn't just restore my physical health; they also nurtured my emotional, mental, and spiritual well-being. But I didn't always live this way. Like many others, I thought success meant pressure and perfection. For too long, I pushed myself relentlessly, trying to "do it all," ignoring the wisdom my body whispered to me. I buried the trauma of the Brace Years deep within, masking the pain with a chip on my shoulder, as if proving my worth to the world would erase my struggles. I abused myself when I lived in full-throttle mode because I failed to truly love myself. This realization was my turning point. My belief system had been flawed, and I didn't understand these things. But now, when I see my reflection, I feel something different—a deep sense of love and honor for the person looking back at me. There is no greater win, no bigger milestone, than truly being at peace with yourself.

My newfound passion turned into a thriving mission. I wasn't just guiding individuals; I was empowering them to reclaim their health, one step at a time. Under my guidance, people felt seen, heard, supported and understood because I knew what it felt like to be lost and in pain.

My professional journey wasn't just about building a business. It was about living my truth and helping others find theirs. The pain I once carried became the foundation for my purpose. Every challenge I overcame strengthened my commitment to guiding others toward their victories.

Now, as Heather Healer™, I am a wellness practitioner who has lived through the battles and emerged stronger. My guiding principle remains: "Wellness is what you do, Health is your result™." It's a reminder that every small, intentional choice matters and that healing is possible for everyone willing to take that first step.

Moderation, I've learned, isn't about limitations—it's about understanding your needs, letting go of guilt, and creating balance. Life's chaos still sneaks in, and I sometimes lose my grip, but those moments don't define me anymore. The difference now is that I have the tools and the self-trust to realign faster.

I'll never forget my darkest day when I made a decision that seemed so small and insignificant—walking to a fire hydrant. One step became two. It was the beginning of everything.

Every choice matters. Everything in life is interconnected. Wellness isn't just preventative—it's healing, too. And your health, for better or worse, is shaped by those everyday decisions. If you're anything like me, striving for optimal health, then good wellness practices aren't optional but essential. It takes time. I didn't get sick in a single day, and I didn't get well in a single day either. Healing is a journey. Everyone's path to optimal health looks different because our circumstances, environment, genetics, and choices shape us.

This is the good news—it's never too late to change. True health doesn't come from shortcuts or "magic potions." It's found in the small moments that collectively define our days.

The Takeaway: Small Steps Lead to Big Change

Healing doesn't happen in extremes. It happens in the in-between, where you rest without guilt, nourish yourself intentionally, and honor your body's needs. Even the smallest steps forward, taken consistently, can lead to something extraordinary.

Your body is resilient, but your spirit is unstoppable. So, what's your "fire hydrant"? Is it a short walk, a nourishing meal, or simply the choice to get up and try again? Whatever it is, take *that first step*. Trust that progress will follow, and remember, community is where true strength lies. We aren't meant to walk this road alone.

To this day, I live with ongoing health challenges, and my back is still a mess. But I live vibrantly because of my wellness practices. I don't just exist—I thrive. And I want that for you too.

Remember my mantra, "Wellness is what you do, health is your result™." It begins with one decision. Start today.

Alexis O'Sullivan

Alexis's friends describe her as a beacon of positivity and resilience—a 'phoenix by nature' who turns challenges into opportunities and embodies an infectious enthusiasm for life, with a smile that lights up any room. Her engaging writing mirrors her energetic spirit, offering warmth, depth, and an underlying positivity in a style that is both captivating and easy to read. Beyond her nursing career, Alexis has authored two children's charity books, channeling her creativity towards making a difference. She is deeply committed to personal growth and has invested heavily in her own development, always striving to be the best version of herself and helping others along the way. Alexis is honored to share her story in support of Hopefull Handbags, and remains devoted to spreading love and light to illuminate the lives of those in darkness.

(scan the QR code to visit Alexis O' Sullivan's FB Page)

https://web.facebook.com/alexis.o.sullivan.3

Shine Your Light

"Let your light shine so brightly that others can see their way out of the dark."
– Katrina Mayer

When I agreed to share my story I was given months to write it but with the deadline a week away I still hadn't written a word. Why not? I couldn't even answer that.

They say if you quieten the mind, the soul will speak but whoever 'they' were, they hadn't met my monkey mind and its ten thousand tangents. I persevered and slowly the doubts began to show themselves. Why would anyone want to hear my story when there are so many better-written stories in the world?

It wasn't even all of my story to tell. What right had I to drag up the ghosts of the past and potentially damage the reputation of the dead and of those who may have since changed their ways?

I was starting to think that sharing my story was coming at too high a personal cost as I could feel myself in danger of spiralling back into the darkness by allowing old tales to trigger me. I sought advice from friends and mentors and the answers were always the same. "Listen to your intuition, Alexis."

Excellent advice but it felt as helpful as a chocolate teapot because I wanted a quick, external fix not more internal soul-searching. I decided the answer was bound to be in one of the countless books I had bought but never read. I am guilty as charged for buying too many self-help books and turning them into shelf help. As I desperately scanned the bookcase, I spotted an old journal I'd forgotten I had started and never finished. I had only written 25 pages but there, on page 11, was everything I needed to be reminded of written by my own hand.

"I don't want to be a passive lighthouse. I want to run back into the flames and pull them out. I remember how that fire hurts and I want to rescue them even if it means I get hurt a little in the process. I control the narrative so I will focus on the light, not the darkness or the pain."

So that only left me with 6 days to write this chapter and while the temptation was there to use A.I to help me, I knew this story had to come from my heart so here goes.

On August 5th 2019, with a trembling hand, I put the key in the lock and opened the door. Until that very moment, I didn't even know bedrooms with Yale locks existed. The room smelled so musty I could taste it, but that sensation was quickly washed away with the salt of my tears. There were a lot of tears that first night and an overwhelming sense of shame. How had I let my life get so low that emergency accommodation was my only option? In hindsight, it was the bravest move I ever made but that's the thing about shame, it succeeds through secrecy and self-criticism clouding your judgement.

I can't go back in time to tell myself it would all work out so instead I'm going to tell whoever needs to hear it today that you are going to be ok and that the best revenge is healing so much that you don't want any. My advice doesn't have a gender in mind so please know that you don't need to stay in situations that no longer serve you. You don't need to try to bash square pegs in round holes or lose yourself, one compromise at a time, trying to please others and you certainly don't need to settle for anything less than you deserve.

It's easier said than done to just leave. Despite everything that happened, it still took me years to get to the place where I felt strong enough to pack my bags and go. When I did, I wasn't prepared for the guilt that hit me. Maybe I should have tried harder to make it work? Maybe all the things he had said were true and the problem was me? Maybe I drove him to say and do the things he did?

Therapy later taught me these thoughts weren't true but at the time I felt like I was failing us both and kept flogging the dead horse down its bare bones.

To give some context I should probably point out that I now found myself waking up in that dingy room with its shared grotty bathroom as a 42-year-old student nurse on the island of Guernsey feeling very distant from my family and friends back home in Ireland. Ironically my ex and I had moved there for a fresh start with our two dogs after a particularly rough patch in our relationship.

I had lost a much longed-for pregnancy and I felt that he sought solace in a bottle. I was two weeks away from finishing my first year of nursing and leaving would have had financial repercussions that I simply didn't feel I was in a position to pay. I decided to stay for a fortnight then fly home to see my father and figure it all out. He would know what to do, he always did. I've been a Daddy's girl from the day I was born. I was like a child counting down the number of sleeps at Christmas to see him. My Dad was just as excited as I was. Although I did not arrive until late on the night of August 20th, he was waiting up to welcome me home with the brightest smile and the biggest bucket of tea. My beautiful special needs sister Camille was sitting beside him on the couch, and we stayed up for hours planning our adventures for my stay.

When my mother tragically succumbed to an alcohol-related injury in 2008, we had become even closer and used to call ourselves the 3 Amigos. I was also blessed with 5 brothers but there was just something magical in our father/ daughter bond that I'm not sure I'll ever find the words to fully express.

I have so many happy memories from that trip. We packed the first few days with seeing lots of our favourite faces. Top of the list were Cathy and Millie, Max's mum and sister. Mighty Max, to give him his full title, was the bravest boy with the cheekiest smile and the sweetest nature. Losing him to cancer the day after his 8th birthday was heartbreaking for all who loved him. I don't think any of us have ever been the same. Although his time on earth was short, his impact was huge. In my case, he inspired me so much that weeks after his death, I applied for nursing school to honour his memory.

It was also to honour Stephanie Knight, another beautiful soul who was taken too soon by cancer. They both featured in the first children's charity book I worked on along with 13 other children only 6 of whom are still alive today. Ava is one of those and she's always held a special place in our hearts because after her cancer treatment finished, she started fundraising to help other families by growing her hair to cut it to create a wig for another child.

Dad and my sister Camille love Ava's family as much as I do so our next stop was the Kingdom of Kerry, in the South West of Ireland, to visit them in Killarney. The photos of that day still light me up as everyone was smiling. They also serve as a stark reminder of how quickly things can change because two days later we got the news none of us wanted to hear, Daddy's cancer was back.

If he was scared he never let it show as he laughed and joked with the consultant and nurses. The next morning at Mass, he felt unwell and instead of a planned shopping trip in town, we took a trip back to the hospital in an ambulance. We arrived together but after 12 long inseparable days (thanks to the staff allowing me to sleep over) I left there alone. I held his hand until it went cold, kissed him on the forehead, and then told him I loved him over and over until they came and took his body to the morgue. It didn't seem real. He had been so full of life, he was my hero, my person, my best pal so when his heart stopped beating it felt like mine did too.

I didn't think my world could get any smaller than it did that day but then came the isolation of the Covid-19 lockdown. By this time I was now sleeping in a single bed in a glorified bedsit with unpainted grey concrete walls on the hospital grounds. I felt utter loneliness, I missed my dad, I missed my dogs, I missed my sister Camille and I missed my friends and family back home in Ireland. I was drowning in a sea of tears by night and desperately trying to keep the bright side out by day.

Camille didn't understand why I couldn't come home to visit and her pleading cries just shattered my already broken heart into even smaller pieces. Because of Covid, it would end up being 550 days before I was able to fly home to see her. My Facebook friends became my life vest and helped me to keep my head above water every time I wanted to give in to the grief.

Through them, I discovered that my salvation lay in service to others as I noticed so many of them were struggling but still showing up to serve with a smile. I threw myself into my studies and took on a part-time job as a healthcare assistant to help out during the pandemic. The first few weeks I was tasked with helping to run the desk at one of the hospital entrances. It took me back to my days as a hospital porter in my hometown in Ireland and jogged a memory of when my Dad was admitted as a day case when I was on duty.

My role that day was to mop any blood from the operating theatre floor, empty the clinical waste bins and roll the patients on their trolleys between recovery and the ward. You would think I was the leading surgeon by the way he was telling anyone who would listen that I was his daughter. He never lived to see me graduate or wear my nursing scrubs but I have no doubt that he is as proud of me today as he was that day as a porter.

My Daddy never cared about what anyone did or what they had as he was all about who they were. Most people don't realise the depths of his good deeds as he rarely spoke about them. He was one of the founding members of the Samaritans in Limerick, Ireland and spent years working in the wet houses of London with the homeless.

In his later years, he was a valued member of Al-Anon, an organisation which supports those struggling with a loved one's addiction. Recalling that precious memory sparked an overwhelming sense of pride and privilege that I was lucky enough to still carry his surname and smile.

Dad's favourite question to ask was, "What do you do if you see someone without a smile? His face would always light up as he delivered the answer "You give them one of yours". This motto became my mission and slowly the tightness in my chest started to ease. I decided my purpose was to allow his light to continue to shine brightly by beaming his smile through mine to the world.

Fast forward to June 5th 2020 and after my fifth move in 2 years, I had made it to a slightly bigger bedsit. Despite an unusually noisy fridge at the bottom of my bed trying to keep me awake I didn't care because it was a double bed and I could stretch out like a starfish if I wanted. I had learned the difference between being alone and being lonely. Despite still feeling a bit Billy No Mates, I found myself repeating the affirmation "I am surrounded by people who love and support me."

Now, I'm fortunate enough to sleep soundly in a king size and that affirmation has become my reality so I count my blessings daily.

Let me bring you back to how I turned my frown upside down.

As I couldn't afford to buy books, I joined the library and found myself drawn to the personal development section. It reminded me of Dad's bookshelves. That man was ahead of his time in so many ways. I found one I liked the sound of "How to be Brilliant" by Michael Heppell and I studied it as if my life depended on it. I now know in many ways that it did.

By August 20th 2021 I had earned a first-class honours degree in nursing and was packing up my dream car to get on the ferry having secured a dream job in a private clinic on another of the Channel Islands called Jersey. My boss flew me back in style on a private plane for my graduation and I had a photo of Daddy and Max under my graduation cap as I walked on stage to collect my scroll from the Dean of the University, Carmel Clancy. In a strange twist of fate, my mother's name was Carmel Clancy before she married my dad. If you knew her, you would be laughing as she loved being centre stage.

As a side note I'd like to share that it still blows my mind to see how far I've come from that library book and bedsit as earlier this year I attended a masterclass with Michael Heppell and his stunning wife Christine in the Chapter House of Durham Cathedral, UK. I also flew to see them for lunch with friends in Newcastle, before flying to London for dinner. Leaving Guernsey before my six-year contract expired meant I had to repay £27,750 in tuition fees and I'm proud to say I made my final payment in

November 2024. I am living the days I prayed for and now I pray that everyone else can find this peace and prosperity too.

The dream car is also worth mentioning because I had been driving a battered secondhand one that had its bumper held in place with coloured zip ties. I dreamed of owning a Fiat 500. I didn't want anything too big on the tiny lanes of small island living. It seemed a pipe dream but it became a reality in the most amazing but bittersweet way. When my dad's Last Will and Testament was read, I found it very hard to come to terms with it for so many reasons. Not least because it all just seemed so cold and final to see his wonderful life broken down into euro and cent. As a result, I didn't chase my share and was slow to respond to the solicitor's letters which I found upsetting as they kept referring to him as the deceased. I did not know that these delays would eventually result in the payment arriving in my account on April 17th. The money was deposited on my birthday on the 16th! Daddy was always buying me silly gifts and often bringing home what he deemed treasures (and I jokingly referred to as tat) but for my birthday it was always cash in a card so I can't express this serendipitous timing. I decided to use the money to buy a car so he could continue to accompany me on my adventures. As I pulled into the very first car dealer, there was a bright shiny blue, soft top convertible, high spec Fiat 500 waiting for me.

I say waiting for me because when I spoke to the salesman, he explained it had just arrived and that it had been a birthday gift from a father to his daughter but she had decided she was ready for something bigger. I bought it on the spot and have never had the desire to drive anything else. This decision became a problem in November 2023. The dream turned into a nightmare when my car was crushed in a storm and the insurance company wanted to write it off. I too felt crushed because it felt like losing Dad all over again. This was a harsh lesson in getting attached to things. I am happy to report that, thanks to my lovely Irish friend Margaret, and a very kind and caring soul at the repair centre the car was saved and restored along with my faith in humanity.

Now to get back on track (you can probably now better understand what I meant in my opening paragraph about my tangents and how even they have further tangents). I'd like to say I arrived in Jersey and lived happily after but the reality was I got lost on my first night, had to sleep on a yoga mat on the floor of my unfurnished apartment for the first few weeks and quickly found myself in a relationship with someone who had a alcoholic ex that subsequently assaulted me on the street so I had to call the police. Wondering how it had all started to fall apart again so fast, I threw myself back into the personal development world. Except this time I didn't just read the books, I immersed myself fully in the material. I invested in courses and mentors which ultimately meant I was investing in myself. I will confess to going through a shiny object stage of flitting from one self-proclaimed guru to the next and at one point I felt like Jack and the Beanstalk, giving away a lot of money, in the hope of receiving the magic beans.

I will save you time and share the secret that you don't need to look outside for the answers because they are already inside you. All you need to do is take the time to listen. My intuition was telling me for years to leave but I kept letting its quiet voice get drowned out by my doubts. As a result of not listening to my intuition, I now have a faint scar on my forehead to remind me of how bad things became. If, like me, you have trouble tuning into the voice within, don't be afraid to ask for help.

However, I would encourage you to take your time and find a teacher you resonate with, then do your due diligence and research them before you trust them enough to spend your time or money. The other thing that completely changed my life was developing an attitude of gratitude and always looking for the good in everything. I credit this to discovering the teachings of the late, great Bob Proctor. I later discovered that he starred in the film version of the best-selling book, The Secret by Rhonda Byrne. My Daddy had given me a copy many years previously.

The parallels to my Dad didn't stop there as I discovered Bob's son Brian had written a book called My Father Knew the Secret. It became the greatest gift I ever received on my grief journey as it finally breathed the life back into my lungs that I felt had left with Dad's last breath. Reading Brian Proctor's tender account of his final days with his father, unlocked a treasure trove of similar memories I must have unwittingly buried with Dad when he was lowered into the ground.

That book is the reason you are reading this chapter today because Brian and his wonderfully wise wife Cory, helped me find my voice. I don't think it's any coincidence that when we finally met for dinner it fell on the exact 5th anniversary of my dad's funeral. When I was struggling with self-doubt and unsure if I could write my story, Cory shared with me that when she had similar doubts, Bob said to her "You have no idea how what you share could help another person. That is why we share our stories so others can learn". Brian's advice about writing was perfect too "Stay authentic, speak from your heart, not your head, share what you know, share what you learned and how you use it".

I'm so grateful for their guidance and am honoured to have been one of the Beta students on their Proctors Principles course. It's brought so many like-minded people into my life and my future looks bright. It would be remiss of me not to thank three of my fellow students Monte Collier, Stephen King and Joanne Laverty who were also instrumental to me finally putting my pen to paper. I'm still happily nursing at the same clinic in Jersey but I've just started taking a professional speaking course and I plan to stand on a stage to help others find their way out of the darkness of death and into the light of legacy.

In the meantime, please know that no matter what life throws your way, you should always remember to shine your light, send it in bright brilliant beams into the world, smile from your soul out, radiate love freely and be a bonfire for people to warm themselves. If you do this, I guarantee that it will find its way back to you in the most life-changing ways. Never forget that your past does not define you and that even if your rock bottom turned out to have a basement, one day your test will become your testimony.

Everything that happens in life can be seen as a blessing or a lesson. Personally, I see it as both because there will always be a silver lining if you look hard enough. My Daddy always reminded me that we are all just walking each other home and every time someone died he would say "another one safely home." Thanks to my faith, I truly believe he is now safely home. Entering into the spirit of walking each other home, I would like to say that if you don't believe in yourself right now please know I'm here for you and that you can borrow my belief in you until you build your own because I know in my heart that you are destined for more.

I started this chapter with a quote so I feel it is fitting to finish with one that may help you to find your voice and share your story.

"One day you will tell your story of how you overcame what you went through and it will be someone else's survival guide."
– Brene Brown.

Orla Kelly

Orla Kelly, an accomplished Irish book publisher and founder of Orla Kelly Publishing, has guided hundreds of clients through the self-publishing journey over the past 10 years, helping them craft professional, high-quality books that resonate with their readers. Orla's passion for her work and personalised approach ensures that every book she publishes reflects the unique voice and vision of its author, making her a trusted ally for anyone considering writing and publishing their book. Whether looking to share your message to attract more clients and grow your business, or have your book as a memoir, sharing your story and leaving a lasting legacy, Orla has your back. Through her innovative programs, including 1:1 support, Orla publishes books that make a real difference in people's lives.

(scan the QR code to visit Orla Kelly's website)

https://orlakellypublishing.com/

How Parenthood Led Me to Rewrite My Life

"Only if you have been in the deepest valley, can you ever know how magnificent it is to be on the highest mountain."
— Richard Nixon

Reaching over my heavily pregnant belly, I gently lifted my sick child from the back of the car. He was covered head to toe in vomit, and as I held him close, I mentally vowed *No more. I'm done. I can't keep going like this.*

My two-year-old son, Michael, had just thrown up, and I was dropping him at the childminder so I could go to work. I worked three days a week as an environmental consultant contracted to another company and had thought I could juggle everything. I'd believed I was invincible, that this relentless pace was what others expected of me.

But the truth was, no one had imposed these unrealistic expectations on me—no one except myself. I had built the prison I found myself trapped in, and only I could break free.

The childminder met me at the car, took one look at me, and said, "Don't worry, he's fine. I have spare clothes. You go." She meant well, but her words hit me hard. Something shifted deep within me.

What was I trying to prove? Why did I feel I had to fit everything into my day and be the perfect mother, wife, and worker? Others seemed to be able to cope. Why not me? The more I pushed myself, the more of a failure I felt. And then Michael got sick with TB from his creche, and the guilt crushed me even more. Even though I had withdrawn him from the creche before it was discovered, when I got a call from the caregivers, I just knew something was wrong. They were informing all their current and past clients that a worker had tested positive and the contamination had spread through the different rooms. Michael was one of the unlucky kids.

He did not bounce back, and his respiratory system was compromised for a long time, meaning lots of infections, medications that brought their own side effects, and hospital and GP visits. Erring on the side of caution became the order of the day. Living in a cool, damp climate didn't make things any easier.

I became a full-time stay-at-home mother when my daughter Emer was born. Money was tight, as we had lots of medical expenses and tried so many alternative therapies and supplements to keep Michael well. I struggled with the worry and responsibility of caring for a sick child who had adverse reactions to medication and did endless research to see what I could do other than try to be the best mother I could while at the same time feeling I was failing miserably. Seeing him struggle to breathe some nights meant I was always on alert, listening; my senses were primed for danger and any change in breathing, coughing, temperature, or overall wellness.

As I found things to improve his condition, like giving him certain supplements, eliminating medicines that I felt did more harm than good, learning different therapies to bring him relief, and buying a trampoline for him to jump on, he became stronger, and as he grew, the damaged parts of his lungs didn't grow to the same extent, so his overall health improved. When I look back now on those days when a consultant said he might have to get parts of his lungs removed, I shudder. Thank God it never came to that.

Being a stay-at-home mum was a decision of absolute necessity for me, one I have never regretted, though there were times I found myself feeling so alone and overwhelmed.

As I learned to slow down, both physically and mentally, I discovered a simpler way of life. Days were spent on the floor building jigsaw puzzles, telling stories, and walking in nature when the weather wasn't too bad. Deadlines and clocks no longer ruled my life. I began to see the world through my children's eyes, and in their company, I began to open up to the world of imagination and creativity.

Little did I know where that would take me until one evening when Michael, who was around nine, began writing a story for his sister Emer about her toy owl. It was bedtime and he still hadn't finished it, so he asked me to take over if he went to bed. I promised I would. I think many weary parents have found themselves at one stage or another agreeing to something to speed up the bedtime process! After tucking the children into bed, I sat down at the table, staring at his handwritten scribbles. As I read his words, I felt overwhelmed. His story was so full of imagination and heart. It was as though I was being invited into his beautiful world, in which a little butterfly who was unhappy with the colour of their wings wanted to fly to the rainbow to change them and a little owl perched on a branch befriended the butterfly at a time where they needed it the most. I saw innocence, magic, imagination, friendship, self-awareness, and self-esteem in that story. How could I possibly rise to the challenge of finishing it? I felt totally ill-equipped, underqualified, and lacking in confidence in my imagination and ability to do justice to what he'd started. Why had I made such a promise? Could I pretend I forgot . . . ? But then I pictured his small face, disappointed, sad . . .

Picking up the pencil, I closed my eyes and prayed for wisdom and guidance on what to do. At that moment, I found myself stepping away from an awareness of what was happening around me and stepping into my inner world, a world filled with possibilities and magical experiences. The continued story began developing in my mind, like shapes emerging out of a swirling fog, the colours becoming more vivid, like I was almost becoming part of the unfolding story, a witness and a participant.

Opening my eyes, I began to write exactly what I saw in my mind. The words flowed as if they were being channelled through me, pulled from the ether. I wrote until my hand ached, stopped to stretch it, then I wrote some more. My shoulders hunched and my hand throbbed till I could write no more. My mind had quietened. Reading back on what I wrote, I realised I had unconsciously woven little life lessons into the story, all told through the eyes of forest animals who had very little interaction with each other and who had forgotten what it was like to live in an enchanted forest where the young took care of the old and the old shared wisdom with the young and where they made their home a magical and beautiful place to live.

On waking, Michael greeted me with, "Mom, did you finish the story for me?" followed by delight when I shared that I had. And so that evening, I read what I'd written as the children's bedtime story. They loved it and asked me to write some more.

So for several nights, I wrote after they went to sleep and would read a new part of the story the next evening, until the tale was complete. "Mom, can you print it out for us?" squealed Emer in delight, holding her toy owl with pride, knowing that he was the centre of the story, a story started some days earlier by her brother Michael, two years her senior.

Without thinking, I found myself saying, "I'll do better than that. I'll publish it in a book." I gasped at the words tumbling out of my mouth, but there was no going back. Michael and Emer had heard every word and shrieked with delight. Their very own book!

What had I just done? I had no idea how to make a book. Where on earth had that daft idea come from? But I had made them a promise and was determined to learn how to make a book, publish it, and print it. So I sat down every night after they went to bed and taught myself just that. It was slow, and it was frustrating at times, as I didn't know where to go for help, but with lots of online tutorials and countless trial-and-error episodes, I finally was ready to hit the "Publish" button on Amazon.

I remember my heart racing, my throat going dry. It was almost like I was expecting there to be a loud, booming voice saying, *What do you think you are doing!*

Instead, the book went through the review stage after I uploaded it, and a few days later, I got a "Congratulations, your book has been published" message. I felt so emotional. I ordered a few copies of the book to give to my kids and a few family members but told no one else. This was all so new to me; I was afraid of someone bursting my bubble.

Once the books arrived, Michael and Emer were thrilled and thought I was famous. I assumed that would be the end of it, but excited kids love to share, and soon the word spread that Michael and Emer's mum had published a book! A real book! The story inspired by Owly and started by Michael had now come to life!

Even after a few months, I had told nobody, afraid of being judged. Who did I think I was? Would I be seen as having notions about myself as an author? I had only written it for my kids and no other reason.

As word spread, Michael and Emer's friends and teachers wanted copies too. Neighbours stopped me in the street, delighted to hear my news, and asked where they could get copies, so I began selling them locally. But I wanted to keep under the radar and not draw any attention to myself. What if people hated it? I wondered. Could I cope with criticism and judgment? I didn't think so. I was so far outside my comfort zone and field of expertise. But kids have no such fears or hang-ups!

My little family project was growing wings, and word started to spread.

Then one day, the local school invited me to read the story to the students. Clutching my book, feeling quite vulnerable, I entered the school, expecting to be directed to a classroom—but no, I was sent to a hall full of children. All of them were waiting for me, eager faces full of expectation and wonder, starting up at me. A published author had come to read to them, and more so, this author was a mum to two kids in the school. Bonus points!

Teachers shushed them to quieten them and get them to settle. My heart was thumping. Could they see it? My throat went dry. Then I looked down and saw my own two children with faces filled with pride, looking up at me. I took a deep breath and began.

Reading with all the emotion I could muster, I shared the very same story I had shared with my own kids every bedtime. I could barely croak the final words—"The End"—when I was met with thunderous applause. In that moment, looking around the room, I finally realised that the story wasn't just for my children—it was for everyone.

That small act of publishing for my kids had now sparked something much bigger and awakened in me a desire to be open to wherever this would take me.

It happened sooner than I expected when a chance encounter at an evening networking event opened another unexpected door for me. In making conversation, I mentioned how I'd taught myself to publish my children's book. I got a very favourable response, and guests there were very interested to hear my story, saying it was a skill others would pay for. I had never considered it as a job. I wasn't used to such attention and thought they were just being polite, but one woman there who worked in PR encouraged me to apply for an entrepreneur program; the only downside was that it was closing the next morning. The pressure was on. I had to have the bones of a business plan down on paper and a clear understanding of my unique selling point (USP) and offering. Qualifying through the different interview stages, sometimes by the skin of my teeth, I was accepted, and that program became the foundation of a business I never anticipated but now deeply love.

Through the program, I began to see what I was doing as no longer a hobby but an asset I had and a skill I had developed where I could now help others become published authors.

My confidence grew with the support I was given, and six months later, my business **Orla Kelly Publishing** was born.

I had no idea how I was going to get clients when I first started, but I soon discovered that there is so much goodwill out there. People I had never met heard my story about how my kids had inspired me to write books, and I was given interviews on the radio and in the print media. Soon, the enquiries started to come in.

I got my first client, then the next, and through word of mouth, my business slowly started to grow. My confidence grew, and I felt needed again in a professional capacity. I had found another role that I could own for myself, and it felt great. I set up a home office with a tiny desk in a box room and got to work when Michael and Emer were at school. My days took on another dimension, and I felt empowered being paid for doing something I enjoyed.

I feel both honoured and humbled, often being the first person my clients show their work to and then helping them fulfil their dream of holding their book in their hands and becoming published authors. I still remember one of my most senior clients, a bachelor gentleman in his early eighties; he had gone to his solicitor to make out his final will, and clutching some printed-out poems, he gifted her with them. When she asked him if he had published any, he sheepishly said that though it was a lifelong desire, he felt foolish at his age and probably would take that unfilled dream to his grave. Through her, he was put in contact with me, and it was such a privilege to step into his world for a while and work with him to get his poetry published. The joy on his face when the books were delivered to him will never leave me. So many wonderful people have come into my life through this gift I feel I have been given, and it has allowed me to become financially independent again, running my own business.

As a publisher I help others bring their stories to life, knowing firsthand the vulnerability and triumph of publishing your first book. Each project is personal to me because I remember the emotions of holding my own book for the first time.

I never want to forget that feeling. It keeps me grounded, focussed and open to being the very best I can be knowing there is always room for growth and improvement.

I have learned so much over the years not just about myself but about the power of words and how they really can touch us at the deepest level. Having a dream of being a published author, seeing your book read and enjoyed by others, whether for entertainment or for the wisdom and learning you want to share with others, is not something to be dismissed. Don't let anyone quench your dream. The graveyard is full of unfulfilled dreams. I see it every day and it breaks my heart.

I never thought I would go from environmental consultant to book publisher and so I remind my children, now 17 and near 20 that as human beings we can reinvent ourselves as many times as we want or need to and to never settle into something that no longer fulfils them. They have the power to change. We all do. I did!

Today, my mission is clear: to transform lives one book at a time. Whether it's preserving someone's legacy, sharing wisdom, or simply creating joy through storytelling, I'm honoured to take my clients through the process.

My journey began with a promise to my children, but it became so much more. It became a life of purpose, creativity, and connection.

So I dedicate my story to you. Whatever message jumps out at you, take it, embrace it and don't look back.

Annette Cashell

Annette Cashell is a Holistic Movement Coach who helps women 40+ get rid of pain and/or build bone health so they can do the things they love. She loves to work with clients who are not looking for a quick fix, are ready to make sustainable change and prefer the holistic approach.

Annette is a certified STOTT Pilates® teacher, Fascial Fitness® Instructor, Buff Bones Instructor®, BoneFit™Trained and is Nutritious Movement® Certified (among other qualifications!). Ex-corporate, she avoided a neck fusion operation and now combines her expertise in Pilates and movement to help women regain their lives with corrective exercises and the environmental changes to support them. She is constantly amazed at the body's ability to heal itself, once it's given the space and guidance to do so.

Annette has spoken on radio, podcasts, and presented corporate wellness webinars. She has also written articles for Thrive Global, Brainz Magazine and featured in Katy Bowman's 'Grow Wild' and the Irish Examiner.

She has lived outside Ireland, in Germany and the USA, for 12 years and is fascinated by how culture affects how we move. She now lives in Dublin, Ireland with her husband and 2 cats and is a mother to two adult children. She's a big fan of monkey bars, house swaps, hiking, learning new stuff and Bruce Springsteen (not necessarily in that order)!

(scan the QR code to visit Annette Cashell's website)

https://annettecashell.com/

Exercise is optional, movement is essential

"If you don't make time for your wellness, you will be forced to make time for your illness." – Joyce Sunada

This is my story of how I freed myself from chronic pain and avoided a neck fusion operation through movement, not exercise, and you can, too.

I had only expected to get an injection from the consultant; I never expected to hear the words "neck fusion operation." Panicking, I countered with, "Surely there were some physio exercises that would help with the debilitating nerve pain I have been experiencing", but the consultant assured me "the operation is the only option", as he had never seen such a severe case of multiple bulging discs before. Of course, there was no guarantee the operation would work, and it would likely limit my ability to turn my head severely. While trying to process all of this information, I was asked, "So, when would you like to book in?" Reeling in shock, I had no time to agree, disagree or even process what had just been said.

The next thing I remember is wandering around the consultant's office. Round and round I went, ending up in front of the same bathroom door again and again, not really seeing or hearing anything. I was in shock and couldn't find my way out of the building! In the end, I went into the bathroom, locked the door and cried anxious, heaving sobs. I knew this diagnosis was far from life-threatening, but it truly terrified me as much as if it were. I was a 47-year-old Pilates teacher, I made my living from physical movement and my own ability to move optimally going forward was now in question. Moving well was my whole life - how was I going to cope without it?

I spent the next few days still in shock, inexplicably cradling my neck all the time, afraid it might suddenly 'break' or become even worse. I felt as if my head was an orange and my neck was a toothpick about to snap! Of course, that wasn't the reality, but that's where my shocked and fearful brain and body led me. The never-ending pain continued alternating between sudden surges of electricity racing down my arm and the constant agonising dull ache of background nerve pain. To feel more supported, I found myself forced to carry my right arm with my left, limiting sitting at all costs and severely limiting any movement with my right hand/arm. I'd already stopped taking the hard-core nerve medications as it felt pointless; they had been making no difference to my pain levels, and I had only been to see the consultant as a last resort. Life felt limited and I felt ancient.

In a twist of fate or the work of the universe, prior to my appointment I had booked to attend a continuing education workshop that very weekend. It was to further my own knowledge to support my clients better. I was still feeling very fragile and seriously questioned if I'd be able to function, not only in my current physical state but also emotionally. I didn't even know if I could continue with my work if I might be unable to move fully in the future. Thankfully, a very good friend encouraged me to try the workshop anyway and in the end, I went. I am so glad I did, as it changed everything.

The workshop I attended after that fateful consultant appointment was centred around working on and understanding "fascia". As a fitness professional, I knew what it was (connective tissue), but I had no idea of the techniques or principles involved in working with fascia. As part of the workshop, the instructor had us complete some interactive sessions. The most powerful one, for me, was one of the simplest. Picture this: a room full of movement instructors spread out in the quiet room, each lying lengthwise on a soft roller (not the regular hard ones you find at the gym). Initially, we just lay there for a while, practising some gentle breathing techniques. Then, we were asked to gently slide ourselves off the roller and to lie directly on our yoga mat and assess how we felt. My brain was already labelling this routine as a monumental waste of time, but, nevertheless, I started to tune into how I felt and… I COULDN'T QUITE BELIEVE IT! I was in shock again, albeit a different kind of shock, an excited and flabbergasted one. I had had no previous expectations, in fact, I had expected to feel precisely nothing. To my surprise, what I did feel was a very real reduction in my nerve pain and, this might sound strange to you, at the same time, the feeling that I was coming back into my body, like I was coming "home."

That experience had been the first sense of relief in over 18 exhausting months of physical and emotional exhaustion. I can't tell you how much this glimmer of hope meant to me! If I could feel some relief and "home-coming" after just a few minutes, surely the effect would improve with time? How much could this positively change my life if I incorporated it more?

I felt elated but also perplexed. How could this tiny intervention have any effect? None of the medications I had been prescribed (including some for epilepsy) had even come close to bringing relief. I quizzed the instructor and came to understand that, although it looked like we were merely massaging our muscles and the fascia around them, this gentle pressure was also having a genuine effect on the nervous system, allowing us to move from "fight or flight" into "rest and digest" mode.

Over the next few weeks, I kept practising the new soft rolling techniques and testing to see if it was just a temporary reprieve. The relief was real and permanent. I was hooked.

I needed to find out all about fascia and the soft rolling techniques. I became obsessed and devoured any research I could find; I was so convinced of the power of this practice, I decided to go to Germany to become certified as a Fascial Fitness Instructor.

Not only was I enjoying the relief from my chronic nerve pain, but I was also able to finally make sense of why it all happened, which provided huge mental relief, too. What had started as acute pain from several bulging discs in my neck had become chronic, as I failed to deal with the stress of everyday life and tried to "just get on with it".

As a result, my nervous system had become hypervigilant to the *perception* of pain. It is similar to an overly sensitive alarm system of a house reacting to every gust of wind instead of just reacting when an intruder breaks in. I learned that there are more pain sensors in your fascia than in any other part of your body, excluding your skin, so rolling fascia makes a lot of sense if you're dealing with chronic pain. Why none of the medical experts had explained this to me before baffled me but I felt blessed to have stumbled onto this technique.

That was 9 years ago. After just a few months of steady improvement, I went from crippling pain and "there's no other option surgery" that could limit my future ability to move and my career as a movement coach and pilates instructor to no medication, no surgery and no pain. My consultant was quite confused and couldn't seem to grasp why I failed to book my neck fusion operation. He kept calling, I kept trying to explain. He was baffled by how I was coping without the surgery; to be honest, it took me a while to truly understand it myself.

Once I had experienced the power of working on the nervous system with soft rolling techniques for my own body, I started incorporating it into all of my classes. I was constantly amazed by the positive feedback from my clients and the reported transformation in their lives. I've included some of their stories (with altered names) below in the hope they can inspire you too!

- Deirdre, a vibrant woman in her 60s, came to me complaining of migraines and anger at the advice she had been given to simply accept them as a "normal part of ageing". Despite years of medical tests and doctors appointments, she had never gotten any relief from the pain. After one private session with me, the migraines diminished and she was then able to maintain this relief using the soft rolling techniques I taught her. Now, she continues to live a full and active life and is a true proponent of dynamic ageing.
- Orla, an indefatigable 50-year-old, was suffering excruciating back and leg pain from 3 unsuccessful back operations. After working with me, she began

- to feel true pain relief for the first time in years. This relief allowed her to start moving more initially and then as she progressed, she was able to resume daily walks and the daily chores we take for granted; her quality of life has improved immeasurably and she feels like she's "gotten her life back."
- Linda, another female client in her 50s came to me with ongoing neck pain that had lasted many years and was blown away by the relief she felt after one soft-rolling session; "life-changing" is the word she uses. She has become a huge fan of soft rolling and continues to use the technique to deal with any neck niggles that arise and to maintain the feeling of well-being in her whole body.

If you're confused - just think SPIDERMAN!

It wasn't just the awareness of the role of fascia on the nervous system that fascinated me. I also became aware of fascia as being a highly interconnected sensory organ, not just covering our muscles but running through them and connecting to form an interconnected fascial web. It is similar to wearing a bodysuit like a Spiderman outfit covering the whole body, including the face, hands and feet. If the fascia is healthy and hydrated, the bodysuit feels "stretchy" and allows the body to move well and be pain-free. If the fascia is unhealthy and dehydrated, then the bodysuit feels tight and restricts movement and/or causes pain.

By extension, working on one part of the fascial web or the virtual Spiderman suit affects other parts e.g. if the sleeves of the body suit were two sizes too small (tight), it would affect how the whole body felt/moved. In my case, I found that rolling my shoulder blades helped my neck pain but rolling the soles of my feet also helped my neck pain. It blew my mind! It also changed my *perspective*; I began to see the body truly as a whole and not just individual parts that needed to be fixed in isolation. Similarly, I began to see how the body couldn't be fixed in isolation without addressing the *environment* in which it lived. I started to wonder how this approach might apply to me.

Even though I was enjoying being pain-free, I was still trying to figure out *why* I had developed such a fragile neck in the beginning. That meant looking at the bigger picture of my life and at first, I couldn't figure it out. I started to look back and realised that even though, by now, I was a Pilates teacher, my body had first started to fall apart in my late 20s.

Back then, I had a "proper job" as a marketing manager in Germany and Silicon Valley, USA. I loved my job, but my body didn't. It started with severe back problems. I was recommended to try Pilates as it was the only exercise that didn't hurt, and I became a total convert after the first class gave me such relief.

I quit my desk job and worked full-time as a Pilates instructor. I continued to exercise more than the World

Health Organisation guidelines. I wasn't overweight or particularly stressed. But the aches and pains continued with carpal tunnel syndrome in my wrist, cartilage issues with my knee and the previously described debilitating issue with my neck.

I was confused. Even though I had given up the desk job and become a Pilates teacher, why was I not thriving healthwise when I was doing everything right? What was the missing puzzle piece?

I hit the books again, reviewed all the research again and finally came across the concept of the "active couch potato"; the term reserved for people who exercise regularly, even every day, even intensely, but are mostly sedentary/sitting for the rest of the day. I hated to admit it, but that was me. I exercised every day and taught 10 classes a week, but *outside* of those "exercise" times, I was as sedentary as the next person. And it turns out - those times outside exercise are equally important.

I retrained as a Nutritious Movement Coach and started adding *movement*, not exercise, into my day, and my body thrived. Small adjustments such as sitting less, standing more, adding more steps to my day, transitioning into barefoot shoes, using a squatty potty, more time outside in nature, reduced screen time, etc.

These small changes started to add up and affected my modern life body. I had already avoided the fusion operation and all the pain associated with it. Now, I was able to maintain that pain-free state with a movement-friendly everyday life to support it. Exercise is optional, but movement truly is essential.

I never expected to end up as a Holistic Movement Coach, but that's the curve ball life threw at me. I'm grateful it ended up like this. I've been able to heal myself several times now, and I've been able to help my family, too.

Whatever the issue, I truly believe a holistic approach works best. You need to address the particular area you're dealing with, but you also need to address the nervous system, for me, that's with gentle soft rolling, and the environment in which the body resides, that's everyday life. As a triple combination, it's incredibly powerful because it addresses the imbalances that modern life creates and inflicts on our bodies and minds. I've seen it again and again with my clients. Plus, I'm living proof.

I know what it's like to live with pain, feel older than your years and the toll that modern living can take on your body. But I also know it's possible to thrive in the modern world without giving up your sitting/desk job or spending hours at the gym.

If any of this resonates with you, don't give up. Modern medicine has a place, but it's not necessarily the first step to address your issues and can often work very well/even better in tandem with alternative medicine. Listen to your gut and get a second opinion. If you decide to pursue the alternative route, take time to choose the correct practitioner. It's your body and you need to feel confident with the person you've chosen to work with.

"Nothing changes if nothing changes." Once you decide to make something happen you need to make the changes to support your choice.

Decide on a small change, even a tiny one, and just do it. EVERY positive change counts. I chose to be honest with myself about how much time I was sitting and worked on reducing it a little at a time. That's the tiny step that started me on the road to whole-body health and pain-free living.

These days, I continue to live this approach and can apply it to any health situation. I've now developed this technique into a signature programme for osteopenia/osteoporosis as this is a condition I am dealing with myself. I'm delighted to say that, using my holistic movement approach, I've been able to reduce my excessive bone loss without using medications and without relying on the usual "just lift weights" mantra.

My approach is always going to be to focus on the whole body. Everything is interconnected, from your head to your toes, from your mind to your body *and* from your body to your everyday living environment. If you're looking for support, I can help you make the changes necessary for sustainable whole-body health so you can get back to doing the things you love and feel like "you" again, just like I did.

15 tips to help alleviate pain and build bone health at the same time:

If you're an excessive sitter, like many modern humans who regularly sit 4 to 8 or more hours a day, then sitting *less* is the number one way to start reducing your pain and building bone health. In practical terms, this means standing more and walking more. It might seem hard to believe that "just" sitting can damage your bones and exacerbate your pain, but the science is clear about "sitting disease" and the ill effects of an overly sedentary lifestyle. Just exercising is not enough to mitigate the risks; the human body is designed to move in small ways, frequently *throughout* the day.

Here's how to make it easy:

1. Use your Fitbit/mobile phone to prompt you to get out of your chair regularly. Ideally, you're getting out of your chair for 1 to 2 minutes every 20 minutes but start with taking a standing break every 60 minutes. Gradually increase the frequency to every 20 minutes.

2. Go for a walk/walk break around the block/down the street. It doesn't have to be long; EVERY step counts! First thing in the morning is best, but you can also walk before/after work (if you don't

have to commute, add in a morning and evening walk as an artificial commute) or add it to your lunch routine to get food/ drink or just consume it outside.
3. Commit to regular walking with a walking buddy; it will make you much more likely to do it when the weather gets cold/wet. Plus, it builds community and connection which are important factors for reducing pain.
4. Meet your friends for a coffee but take it to go and do your catching up while walking. Again, it doesn't have to be for long; even adding in a short walk before/ after meeting your friends makes a difference.
5. Use public transport when you can; it usually involves more walking than driving, especially if you add in some standing while on public transport. You don't have to stand the whole trip; every little bit counts to reduce total sitting time.
6. While using public transport, get off a stop early to add in some extra steps.
7. Ditch the car to do errands if you can walk there instead; if you can't walk the whole way, drive part of the way and walk the rest.
8. Park further away from the shops in the car park and walk the difference.

9. Decide on some routes that you usually drive, that could be walked instead and promise yourself to only walk there from now on e.g. to a friend's house.
10. Use natural breaks as cues to move e.g. toilet breaks, getting some water breaks, getting an eye break by walking to a window and looking outside. One guide is to look at something 20 feet away, for 20 seconds, every 20 minutes so you can easily combine it with a standing break.
11. Use household chores as "movement opportunities" e.g. whenever the dishwasher/washing machine needs loading/unloading, whenever the washing needs to be hung up/taken down, or when laundry needs to be folded (I can see a laundry theme here!), bins need to be taken out, you get the idea. You're sprinkling housework throughout the day, instead of doing it all in one go to decrease your total sitting time and getting your work/housework done at the same time.
12. Use "nuisance" interruptions to get you moving e.g. cat/dog needs to be let out/let back in, post-delivery worker is at the door, courier needs a signature. I'm not saying you'll look forward to interruptions but why not get some benefit out of them?

13. Stand up and walk when doing your phone calls. Take them outside if you can for the extra health benefits of daylight and temperature and nervous system regulation which helps with reducing pain.
14. Check your emails while standing up with your desktop on the kitchen counter/ table at eye level and your wrists at counter level. Use a box to get the correct height for the desktop. The aim is NOT to stand all day but to alternate between sitting and standing.
15. Start all Zoom calls standing up; again, the aim is to switch between sitting and standing. Prof Alan Hedge, Cornell University[2], recommends sitting for 20 minutes, standing for 8 minutes and stretching for 2 minutes in a 30-minute cycle. Standing at the start of a Zoom call for 8 to 10 minutes is a great place to start. Ease yourself in by standing for 3 to 5 minutes at first and then gradually increase to 8-minute standing breaks.

This chapter is dedicated to my little blister, Lara.

---

2 https://ergo.human.cornell.edu/CUESitStand.html

Brigid Stapleton

Brigid Stapleton is a health and wellness advocate empowering others on their journey to optimal health.

Thirty years ago, Brigid opened an organic hair salon and after the birth of her last child 24 years ago and on the advice of her oncologist, she was advised to retire from hairdressing.

She decided to become more involved with health and wellness after facing burnout and illness.

She pivoted her business from hair styling to health and wellness and now empowers others to achieve their lifestyle goals mentally, physically and emotionally, so everyone can live their lives to the fullest.

(scan the QR code to visit Brigid Stapleton's website)

https://thealoeveraco.shop/

From a dark terrifying moment to a magnificent triumph

"Hardships often prepare ordinary people for an extraordinary destiny." – CS Lewis

My legs went out from under me as I slid, slowly and helplessly to the floor of the hospital bathroom. I had fully intended to be sick in the toilet, but my legs defeated me. I had just heard the words "aggressive cancer" from my oncologist. This day was my darkest, most terrifying moment. It was a Sunday morning two days after I had a radical mastectomy, with drips and drains still attached. I was shocked because I had lots of tests and scans the week prior, and everything seemed good. They wanted to be sure it had not travelled to any other part of my body, but unfortunately, one tumour was resting on my breast bone and the surgeon told me they had had to shave the top layer of the bone to remove all of it. I'm so glad he did. I never thought that day would come when I would be thankful my breasts and part of my breast bone were removed.

To set the scene, let me take you back to a few weeks prior, with a four-month-old baby and four other children at home to care for. I was having a lot of breast pain, so I contacted my GP by phone, thinking I needed to be seen and get an antibiotic, possibly for what I thought was mastitis. He didn't ask to see me, saying I had probably just pulled a muscle in my underarm, yet I had this niggling gut feeling that wasn't quite what was going on. Thankfully, I didn't let it go, so I called the hospital. With a stroke of luck or intervention from the universe, the person who answered the phone happened to be a Breast Health Nurse. I explained what I was experiencing, and after answering her questions, she advised me to come in as soon as possible for a breast check. She told me it was a coincidence that she answered the phone, as she had been passing the office when the phone rang, and someone called out and asked if anyone could 'answer that phone', and so she did. She felt it was a sign she was to talk to me that day. She asked me to come in the following Monday, but as we'd already booked a trip away, I went in just over a week later instead and had a mammogram.

Did you know that young breast tissue appears white on a mammogram? I hadn't, but I soon learned this and much more. Because I had recently given birth, my breast tissue was more pronounced due to hormone levels and activity in the breast. They couldn't see anything on my mammogram, but the physical exam proved that I had three quite significant lumps. A needle aspiration removed fluid from one of the lumps, confirming a cancer diagnosis. When I was told the news they would need to remove my breast, I told them to take whatever they needed as I had to be around for my family, especially my new baby.

It was after my doctor's departure that the shock and profound realisation set in, and I slid to the bathroom floor, crying and shaking with shock. Eventually, I made my way back into my bed, dazed and exhausted. When my brother Anthony arrived, he held me in his arms while I sobbed and told him how scared I was. He was like a Dad to us all, as he was the eldest.

The following day, while in my hospital bed, I was informed I would need a skin graft.

I told the consultant I did not have time for this as I had a new baby to look after and he said that the team would be around later to talk. Little did I know what I was in for. They came back later when my husband was there, and I was told there was not much hope and that giving me chemotherapy would only increase my chances of survival by 20%. I sat there, frozen, just watching mouths move and not hearing any sounds. My mind was closed off to the reality of being so ill. I pulled the curtain closed around the bed, closing off the outside world. Somehow, I managed to get dressed and left the hospital with my brother.

As the realisation set in of what I faced, my first thoughts were for my children, family and extended family.

My beautiful, bouncing baby girl, Jess, was just four months old then. As she grew up, Jess was quiet but able to read situations. She is more vocal now at twenty-five, rules the house, and can do nothing wrong in her dad's eyes. I'm constantly saying I'm changing my name to Jess to get what I want.

My cheeky Katie was only seven at the time. She was supposed to be called Pearl. We even had "Welcome home Pearl" banners for her in the house, but she looked like a Katie. When she was born, she was sucking her fist as she arrived into the world. She was a wild child but loving. Her sensitive and determined spirit led her to become a social worker.

At the time, Aimee was only fourteen, a young teenager. It was already hard enough to be a teenager without this. Aimee's name means fit to be loved. She has carried more than her share of responsibility and burden. She is graceful, kind, and pragmatic. She is a great big sister to my other two daughters and a loving aunty to my eldest granddaughter.

Jonathan was the eldest, nineteen at the time of my diagnosis. He is a sensitive and positive soul and thought that nothing bad would happen, but it did. He is now a sports journalist.

And of course, there was my eighteen-year-old nephew, my brother's son, Ludovic, whom I have cared for since he was three, and I raised him alongside our own four children. Ludovic inherited his gentleness and sensitivity from his mother, who worked as a PA for Pavarotti. Incidentally, Pavarotti sent me a white scarf on which he drew a heart signed by him, but unfortunately, it never got to me. It's nice to know he did. He lost his mother in 2016 and was an only child. It was the saddest funeral I had ever attended.

My greatest worry during this time was for my wonderful husband Jimmy. He almost went grey overnight with stress and anxiety.

My mind was in a tailspin. Aggressive Cancer: Who would take care of my children, especially baby Jess? How would my husband manage on his own? I was in despair.

After the news, my husband stayed to sign the relevant papers on my behalf. I could not do it. When I got home, I held my three girls. We all cried together, not because I had cancer but because I was losing my hair. The very thing I had built my livelihood and passion around as a hairdresser. Of course, we were not just crying because of the hair, but also because we had never heard of anyone surviving cancer 25 years ago. In the movies, when someone lost their hair, they always died; that was what scared them. As I told more people my news, I tried to lighten it by sharing how I was getting more upset about losing my hair when I was possibly dying from cancer.

My next thoughts went then to my siblings. The news had yet to be shared with them. As a family, we had buried another brother, John, a few years before. He was a teacher and died at age forty. He was four years older than me, and his death made my prognosis very real. We had already been through so much. How could I tell them?

John was handsome and popular with the ladies. He would visit the hair salon where I worked as a young stylist in Dublin. The girls would swoon over him. I used to be mortified, thinking, 'Why on earth are they swooning over John?' I mean, who thinks their brother is handsome? Most times, he was a pain in the neck, checking out any boyfriend I had and frightening some of them away.

As I was contemplating how my siblings would take the news, I thought back to the morning he died. He looked out the window and said he would love to walk barefoot in the grass. John knew he was ill, and that he was going to leave us soon. Because he hadn't the strength to do it, I went outside to walk barefoot in the grass for him. I still remember feeling the grass, feeling the pain in my heart, and hearing the bells from the Church for Sunday mass. He was the first sibling to die, and it was a terrible loss for his son and partner as well as his three sisters and six brothers. What if my family and siblings had to go through this again with me? I could barely face the reality of this myself, let alone put my family through it again.

"We must accept finite disappointment but never lose infinite hope." Martin Luther King, Jr

I kept asking myself "Why why why me? What got me here?"

I tried to rationalise the diagnosis, but I had a million questions racing around in my brain.

I wondered if it was the stress of an abused childhood. I felt I was always living in fear every day and night. When my brother died, I found the courage to confront my abusers. I did not want it to continue and wanted to protect my children. I've since learned that my fear and thinking negatively caused the stress hormone cortisol to rage through my body, which may have been a contributing factor to my illness.

A few weeks after I left the hospital, I was in a lot of pain. I had been using aloe vera gel in the salon for burns and grazes, and I knew it was good for pain, so I began applying the gel topically to help with the skin sensitivity and the pain on my graft. I never imagined the chain of positive events this would set in motion in my life. Six weeks later, I went to see my oncologist, red-faced and embarrassed for having made an abrupt exit from my hospital bed some weeks previous to this, when he gave me the bad news.

He examined me carefully, and proclaimed, with surprise and delight that I had new pink skin forming just like a baby's bottom. This time I remembered his words clearly. He said, "You don't need your skin graft." He was astounded at my progress and how much my skin had healed in such a short time, after my radical mastectomy. He even then asked for some of the same aloe vera gel that I used on my skin.

I was placed on a clinical trial for almost a year that had five different rounds of chemotherapy. The chemotherapy left me with a lot of side effects, one being medical menopause. How is this possible when I still had the physical effects of being pregnant, like sore breasts? I went into the hospital at the age of forty-three, and after a year of treatment, I felt like a ninety-year-old woman with a one-year-old baby. It was a really strange time. My mother had more energy than I did. Eventually, my oncologist told me I would have to give up the hairdressing. I had lymphoedema and fibromyalgia, and I was going in daily for bandaging of the lymphedema to try to help reduce the inflammation. It was hard even to lift a kettle at the time. The doctors felt that repetitive use of my hand when doing daily cuts, colours and blow-dry's, amongst other things was undoing the benefits of the treatment they were offering me. The thing I loved, and my incredible journey of having opened the first organic hair salon in my little Clondalk Village in Dublin, was going to have to end for health reasons. It was heartbreaking.

It was my passion and I worked at it for almost thirty years, successfully building my business. What else could I do?

As I was winding down my business, I found myself confiding to a client called Phill who also happened to be a friend. She suggested I look at a business she was involved with, but I declined as I was too ill then. A week later, she called me and said, "Brigid, I can't stop thinking about you and the situation that you are in. Would you be willing to look at this business for the benefit of your health and your income? It was an aloe vera based company. I was already looking for more aloe vera gel at the time and Phill talked me through the business plan. Even though I was still very ill, I joined the company because it made sense to me. I needed something else to focus on and felt I had nothing to lose and everything to gain. I was nervous, but she believed in me, and with her help and support, I decided to go for it. The business training and support provided led me to great heights. I am so glad to this day that Phill thought of me, and I know she was praying for me, too, and still continues to do so. A lovely lady. Thank you, Phill. I'm in great debt to you.

"Sometimes the strength within you isn't a big fiery flame For all to see.
It's a tiny spark that whispers so softly
Keep going you've got this." – Author unknown

"A fire begins with a flame even a smouldering one." – Unknown author

And so a new chapter in my life began. I opened my 'business box' with great excitement and trepidation at the same time. Inside, I found lots of great information, but the most significant change came when I started drinking pure aloe vera gel. It changed my life. I felt physically, mentally and emotionally better and stronger. I began to read self-help books and began to change my thinking. The first one to make an impact was a book about 'excusitis' where I realised I had the power to change my circumstances. This felt so empowering. I stopped listening to the negative voices or worrying about what other people thought. I wanted to be authentic but authentic to myself first. To be true to yourself is so empowering.

Our greatest asset in the world is our mindset.

I was privileged to go on a company trip to Dallas, Texas, USA and remember feeling so emotional on visiting one of the aloe vera plantations. As I walked out into the desert field and sat among the aloe plants, I thanked God and reflected on that dark, terrifying moment in the hospital when I slid to the floor.

I was here, alive, going to a rodeo, line dancing, and best of all, sitting on Bobby Ewing's actual bed from the drama series *Dallas*. I was snapped out of my daydream when I heard Rex Moughan, the founder of the aloe vera company, shouting, "What is that lady doing in the desert sun?"

Life seemed wonderful then. I could not believe I was sitting at the pool on the set of South Fork, Dallas, Texas, sipping on a glass of wine. In all the years I watched *Dallas* on television at home in Ireland, I never imagined that I could get an opportunity to visit in person.

Later that day, I tried to explain to Rex how my life had so drastically changed, but tears came instead of words, and my emotions overcame me.

On a later trip to Singapore, I got my chance to speak to Rex and tell him about my personal journey of healing and health improvements through the work I did in personal development and looking after myself through the products.

The next day, he came to me and said, 'Brigid, do you know I went to sleep with a smile on my face last night and thought, that's what this company is all about.'

> *"Laughter is timeless, imagination has no age and dreams are. forever."* –Walt Disney

In 2015, I tragically lost my beloved brother Anthony. The stress and trauma of his passing ultimately led to me suffering a heart attack. During the extensive tests and close monitoring, my heart appeared completely healthy, with no apparent reason for the attack. While trying to uncover the cause, one doctor approached me and asked if I had recently experienced anything particularly traumatic. I initially replied 'No'. He then enquired if anything significant and distressing had occurred the year before, and it was in that moment I made the connection—it had been 9 months since Anthony had died, and the experience had been deeply traumatic for me.

The doctor explained to me that Broken Heart Syndrome is a real condition, known medically as stress cardiomyopathy or Takotsubo Syndrome. He diagnosed me with this condition, as the overwhelming grief and heartbreak of losing Anthony had caused my otherwise healthy heart to have an attack.

I've now grown a global business with the aloe vera company. My favourite country to visit is Bangladesh. I had the opportunity to visit when the office opened there to support the setting up of the brand, and I travelled every year since the opening of the office in 2010 until 2019 when Covid hit. After being there and seeing the poverty and exploitation of women and girls, my vision is to have an orphanage for girls. I don't believe there is one solely for girls yet.

Interestingly, I connected with a lovely man on social media when he commented on something I had shared about Bangladesh. It turned out he was a judge there. Over time, we became good friends, and we planned to collaborate on opening the orphanage for girls and he hoped to gift me the land. He had already opened orphanages in the past but only for boys which are still running to this day, but sadly, he passed away during Covid. I've missed him terribly on a personal level but his loss also means the plans have yet to come to fruition.

What changed me from a quiet, shy person to speaking on stage to thousands? A decision. I decided to change my mindset. Books played a big part. When you read what others overcame and made a success of their lives, ask yourself, 'Why not you?' Work on personal development and believe in yourself. It takes time and action, but it's worth it. I worked on myself more than my work.

You can change your life by changing your thinking. As my husband often quotes Henry Ford, who said, "The battle is won or lost in your mind. If you believe you can you are right, and if you believe you can't, you are also right."

The secret is to find someone who believes in you before you believe in yourself. Read motivational books. One that helped me a lot is *The Power of Positive Thinking* by Norman Vincent Peale. Look at others who have done it and emulate them because success leaves clues.

My passion is to help people believe in themselves. It can change your whole life. Believing in yourself involves learning from your mistakes and developing a healthy and positive mindset. Face your fears as the letters FEAR can be represented as **F**alse **E**vidence **A**ppearing **R**eal. Focus on things that are good and speak only of good. Surround yourself with positive, like-minded people.

> *"I believe in pink. I believe that laughing is the best calorie burner.*
> *I believe in kissing, kissing a lot,*
> *I believe in being strong when everything seems to be going wrong.*
> *I believe that happy girls are the prettiest.*
> *I believe that tomorrow is another day.*
> *I believe in miracles."* – Audrey Hepburn

The main reason I got to where I am today was to break a cycle and to stay alive for my husband and my family. I knew I needed to change my mindset.

I came back from the brink of death and despair in that dark, terrifying moment to magnificent triumph and I'm only getting started.

> *"Wherever you are in life believe in yourself. And still, I rise."* – Maya Angelou

I learned to write my vision down on paper; having that in front of me helped me become determined to reach my goal. My biggest goal was to be healthy in mind, soul, and body. I made a decision to be happy. When you're faced with a life-threatening illness, it changes your perspective on life, and you realise life can be a wonderful gift, just like in one of my favourite songs, "What a Wonderful World" by Louie Armstrong.

One thing that struck me while lying in the hospital bed was that life is a gift life is a gift.

To wrap up, I want to take you to the present day; it has not been easy these last few years as I was diagnosed with post-menopause atrophy. I had my womb and ovaries removed a couple of years ago and this left me with atrophy. It took me a couple of years to discover as I was attending my GP querying if I was getting urinary tract infections or was something else going on? It was through social media I discovered I had atrophy and needed estrogen cream, but my breast care doctor said I could not go on it. I was sent to my oncologist gynaecologist, who was a woman, and she diagnosed me with severe atrophy and said it was relatively safe for me to go on it. When she handed me the prescription, I could have kissed her. The first time menopause was chemically induced due to my radical chemotherapy, the second time it was naturally at age 50, and the third time at post menopause, which led to atrophy. A lot of women are suffering from atrophy and don't know. I take supplements to help as well with this problem.

More recently I had another scare, and this resulted in many weeks of scans. But life is different now. I firmly believe this is due to the community, skills and business I have built, where I have both the experience and the tools to support my mind and body on any journey.

I'm now in the process of buying a property in Italy. I will be travelling to Bangladesh again to help grow the business there. From Bangladesh, I will travel to Pakistan where a colleague intends to join the company and help me form an orphanage. He currently helps free children from childhood labour, from his personal funds. He is a very determined man and his kindness and generosity know no bounds

Everyday life activities also keep me busy including looking after my family. I believe it's important to have fun and dance, smile and laugh often. My Fridays are dedicated entirely to fun. I do hair for fun and have dinner with clients and family. I believe in the power of prayer. I believe in the living word of the Bible.

We all have great untapped abilities and determination within ourselves. My mother always told me I was determined in an annoying tone as if I was doing something wrong. When I was a child, I always thought I was doing something wrong or it was a bad trait to have, but I now think differently

I'd like to leave you with positive things that really helped me and in turn can help you. I turned things around even after a chronically abused childhood.

1. Believe in yourself. Start by loving yourself. Life is precious.
2. Read or listen to self-help books.
3. Follow your instincts as we as women have that ability.
4. Face your fear and do it anyway. Fear is False evidence appearing real.
5. Live today like there is no tomorrow. Live in the moment. Enjoy today.
6. Laugh a lot, as it's good for the soul and increases serotonin. Smile.
7. Be authentic, as it is very powerful when you do. To be true to yourself is empowering.
8. Allow time for fun in your life.
9. Pray, as I believe we are all spiritual beings. The best living book you can read for direction is the Bible.
10. Think on things that are good and give thanks for the blessings in your life.

Contact brgdstapleton@gmail.com

Ewa Wiko

Ewa Wiko is a soulful Reiki Master and painter, embracing femininity and harmony through art and healing. She is a passionate seeker of nature's wisdom, a forest dweller at heart, and a modern-day witch attuned to the rhythms of the earth. She guides women on their journeys to find harmony in body and life.

Art Catalogue:

https://www.whatsapp.com/catalog/353857798861/?app_absent=0

(scan the QR code for Ewa's Instagram account)

@EWA_WIKO_ART

https://www.instagram.com/ewa_wiko_art/

Paintings of Power

"Joy is the simplest form of gratitude."
– Karl Barth

It was a cold, cloudy Sunday morning. It rarely happened that she had time just for herself, so she decided to go to the sea. A walk along the stony beach, the sound of the waves, and the water churning among the stones... there was something magical and soothing in it. After a short walk, she decided to warm up in a local café with a view, sipping hot coffee and enjoying her favourite carrot cake. "Wonderful," she thought.

She stood up eventually, headed for the exit when she felt pain, the first, sharp attack. The pain tore through her body from her lower abdomen, all the way to her lungs. She could barely catch her breath. Each step felt like another stab of a sharp knife inside. She looked around, seeing passersby, families, couples, all smiling, cheerful, full of life... and then there was her. She felt as though she was dying, invisible, and no one saw, no one could help. Worse, she felt she shouldn't ask for help because, as she'd heard for so long, this was just her "nature." But was it? What beauty is there when your own body is fighting against you?

That was me. It was a beautiful, free Sunday morning for me, one year after my confirmed endometriosis came back. I remember that day vividly because it marked a turning point in my healing journey.

After the doctor informed me that my endometriosis had returned, and once I processed the disbelief, fear, and helplessness, I declared war. A war, first and foremost, against Western medicine. I refused to live a half-life. I began searching. The only solutions offered by conventional medicine were hormonal drugs that interfered with my body's healthy function, another surgery or pregnancy.

None of these options were acceptable to me; they even angered me. Live my whole life pregnant? Constantly recovering from surgery? Hormones can mess up one's identity entirely. This was not what I wanted. Deep down, I knew there had to be something more.

I began to search for an alternative, non-invasive path to health. Deep inside, I felt I needed the gentleness of healing, not the sharpness of a scalpel.

One of the first approaches I encountered was Reiki, the study of intelligent life energy, originating from a Source, which could dissolve energy blockages and restore harmony when invited into the body.

I completed Level 1, then shortly after, Level 2, and began practising daily on myself and occasionally on my son. It was incredible to feel the flow of energy and to perceive it, almost as if with an inner vision.

I also started to live according to the five principles of Reiki:

1. Just for today, do not worry.
2. Just for today, do not anger.
3. Just for today, be kind to others.
4. Just for today, work diligently on yourself
5. Just for today, be grateful.

I incorporated regular meditation, breathwork, grounding, nature walks, hikes, and a special diet into my life.

I absorbed vast amounts of knowledge and implemented everything I felt aligned with. Unfortunately, did not see any physical changes in my body, at least not the miraculous results I had been promised.

Despite feeling calmer and happier, my body continued to scream. I felt caught in a loop, wanting to believe the practices were working but questioning it because the results just weren't there. The pain persisted, and the lump in my abdomen was still tangibly felt.

This lack of results led to frustration; frustration with Western medicine, frustration with alternative medicine, and, most of all, frustration with myself. I thought, "It must be me; I must be doing something wrong; maybe I am not doing enough."

All this unfolded behind the scenes of a smiling woman who seemed to have it all together; balancing life as a single mom, an excellent full-time employee, a daughter, a sister, and a friend.

My stubborn self didn't tell anyone about the recurrence of my endometriosis. I didn't want to burden anyone or worry them, as everyone has their own problems. I also feared a lack of understanding regarding my choice of meditation over surgery. I worried that some of my loved ones would think I was crazy and try to pressure me to have the surgery. I worried about judgment and misunderstanding.

However, that fateful Sunday, my body showed me that energy work alone wasn't enough. That day, for the first time, I turned to hormonal pills, and only a combination of them with strong painkillers brought some sort of relief, just enough to survive that day, and the next one.

It was the day I let go of my expectations and, standing vulnerably in front of the mirror, admitted, "I need help."

I stopped being angry at medicine and acknowledged it as a tool that, combined with additional practices, could bring the miracle I longed for.

I know that was the moment I shed my pride and opened myself to new possibilities.

That day, I also decided to care for my body holistically, on all levels.

Shortly after, I found a specialist in bio-resonance therapy, Chinese medicine, and naturopathy and she was just 20 minutes from my home. A miracle!

Together, we began a year-long journey to repair my digestive system, which was in a state of chaos. It wasn't until years later that I learned endometriosis is often linked with irritable bowel syndrome or IBS, something I'd struggled with for a long time.

I started supporting my body with herbs. For the first time, I harvested nettles and made my own fresh nettle juice. I walked barefoot on the grass every day. I drank Chinese herbal teas and various brews to strengthen my stomach and intestines.

I began to feel better, realising that combining energy work with physical body support was an excellent choice.

My journey didn't end there; it was just the beginning of a deep dive into my true self. I began working with a spiritual teacher on feminine energy and womb awakening. I felt an intense desire to learn about my body, understand myself, and truly listen.

I will never forget the week following my first energetic session when, seemingly out of nowhere, I began crying uncontrollably. Tears flowed freely – while dressing, showering, eating – as if a dam had burst. A dam that I built myself from a fear of being hurt.

This process of healing and self-discovery continues to this day, helping me embrace my journey and inspire others to embark on their own paths toward health, happiness and fulfilment.

I knew there was something deeper there, and I wanted to find out what it was.

The womb-awakening program lasted nine months, nine months of diving deeply into my femininity, my sense of being a woman, uncovering and healing blocks I had often imposed on myself. After all, being a woman can feel painful, shameful, uncomfortable, etc.

During the process, I not only learned about my body all over again but fully accepted it.

I will never forget the day I stood naked in front of a mirror, looked at myself from head to toe, and said, "Wow, you are one sexy woman!"

I was in love with myself, my amazing body in its fullness.

I never imagined this journey would be so liberating.

I gained self-confidence and an immense sense of peace that radiated from me.

I remember after meeting a friend for coffee, I received a message: "How do you do it? You're so calm, I admire you for that, and I wish I could feel the same."

That was the first time a small thought crossed my mind, what if I could help other women? A tiny, innocent, almost unnoticeable thought.

In my self-healing journey, I learned that it's worth trying and learning from others. That's how I discovered fasting and castor oil therapy. Both which I still use in various ways to this day, knowing they will remain with me for a long time.

I opened myself up to trying new things and embracing possibilities. I replaced "I would never" with "What if it works?"

That's how I stumbled upon painting. Painting came to me in the most mysterious and magical way. Every time I talk about it, I get goosebumps.

During one process of self-discovery and uncovering my potential, I visualised my amazing future self, the fulfilled, joyful, successful version of me. I had the chance to ask her for advice or a tip on how to get closer to where she is. She didn't say anything; instead, she handed me a paintbrush and walked away.

I didn't understand—what was I supposed to do with that?

I don't paint! I've never been gifted artistically, art was never my dream, and I didn't even have a single painting hanging on my walls.

So, what was I supposed to do with a paintbrush?

I left it alone because I didn't understand it, but subconsciously, it was brewing, growing louder each day. "Try."

I started searching for something I could try without committing to years of art school. I felt a loud "Nooo, not academic painting!" inside me.

That's how I discovered doting; painting with dots and ordered a starter kit. It turned out pretty well, but something was missing—it lacked fire. It felt a bit like a colourful Excel sheet. As a 20-year accountant, I felt it wasn't the path for me.

One evening, while making holiday cards, I had some leftover paint that I didn't want to waste so I grabbed a small canvas I had bought weeks ago. It was waiting for me.

Hmmm..... The first sound of wet paint touching the canvas sparked a fire in my body. It was like lightning shooting through my body from my womb to the top of my head.

I jumped back from the table in shock, internally shouting, "What was that?"

Thank God no one was home.

It was something I had never felt before, like an explosion of heat. Strangely, I wasn't scared; it was pleasant and surprising and felt sooooo ME.

I knew this was it, the missing piece of the puzzle.

That's how it started. It wouldn't leave me alone, so I began asking myself, the Universe, and God what to do next. I didn't want to attend long art schools, nor did I want precise painting. I needed to express freedom, I wanted to feel free while painting. Through meditations, prayers, and dreams, I envisioned the first three paintings I was meant to create and hang in my living room: red, green, and blue, symbolising the root, heart, and throat chakras, respectively. As I write this, I'm looking at them, smiling. They accompany me daily, helping me feel safe, opening my heart, and speaking my truth.

The first time I experienced the energetic power of my paintings was a few months later when I shared the news of my first exhibition in a workshop group. I showed pictures of my paintings, most of which were created using a pouring-paint technique. This method can surprise you. You don't always know the outcome, and it brings childlike joy to the process. One of these paintings had spoken to a beautiful woman from Italy. She wrote to me, "I don't know what's in this painting, but I have goose-bumps every time I look at it. I want it. I need it."

It was the first painting I sold—the first to evoke such a strong reaction in someone. Could there be something to this?

My paintings became part of my life, accompanying me through emotional moments. I paint when I'm angry, heartbroken, joyful, or celebrating. When I don't paint for long I get itchy fingers, it's calling me.

I never stopped learning about myself. I feel there's still so much to discover, and I am likely to be in learning mode for the rest of my life.

On this journey, I began a coaching qualification, which led me to transformational coaching. I decided to help women find harmony in their bodies and lives. I know I succeeded. I wasn't entirely free from endometriosis yet, but I managed to reverse 90% of it. I knew that stepping into the role of guiding others would also help me heal more and more each day.

I still felt something was missing. I loved witnessing my clients' transformations and the feeling of making a difference. I sought guidance again, and the answer came, I had to include my paintings as a healing medium in my sessions.

OMG, I was terrified! My mind went wild. "How? What? Where? I haven't finished any school! I don't have any paper! Painting is like a joyful play for me, how can that be used for healing?"

It took me a while to settle into the idea, but again, "What if it works?"

The chakra healing painting collection was born. I've used it many times in individual and group sessions already, and I'm still learning how to use it best.

What I know is that when someone opens their heart, anything is possible.

Women have dreamed about my paintings before and after sessions—feeling their energy even before experiencing them. That's the best proof for me that this works.

I don't know where I'll be in five years or even next year, but I'm open to possibilities because "What if it works?"

I truly believe we are creators of our reality, life, health, and prosperity.

I stand here to empower women.

Believe in yourself.

Seek help and guidance, don't face your worries and struggles alone. Find your tribe.

I am now 90% free from endometriosis, a disease labelled incurable and chronic. I'm ready to come off my medication, closely watching and listening to my body. I'm eager to learn how to support my body even better.

If you're reading this, I want you to know that you can too.

You just need to decide that this is what you want and open yourself to the possibilities that will come.

My story is to be continued, as is Yours.

Be happy!

Be healthy!

This chapter is dedicated to Ewa, Thank you for not giving up.

Sophia Norley

Sophia, as a small child was trapped by fear, shame and guilt, which she carried around in an invisible but very heavy backpack. It was beyond exhausting and she unknowingly carried these negative emotions into adulthood and allowed them and others to keep her trapped, albeit in a different situation with a different jailor.

As with many who have suffered abuse and neglect in childhood, Sophia attracted someone who found it necessary to control and cause pain. While in this new cage, even more sadness and pain were squished into the already bulging sack that she carried as she tried to navigate motherhood and adult life in general.

It took time, courage and becoming way too close to breaking for Sophia to face the darkness that had engulfed her life and that was still holding her prisoner. She began to unpack her traumatic story, paragraph by paragraph. With each emerging paragraph, more memories came to light, which had been buried for a lifetime. During this process 'Escaping Bohemia' was born and this memoir beat many other biographies to secure the number 2 slot in the Amazon biographies section, not bad for a child that couldn't read and spell.

Throughout this journey, she learnt to love herself as she held the little girl she once was, slowly releasing her from the claws of guilt and shame. During this time she had to make some difficult choices and dramatic changes to her life, as she bravely accepted how she had allowed others during her adult life to continue to mistreat her.

She has now freed herself from chains that once held her so cruelly and tightly and continues to share her story and first-hand wisdom in any way that she can, as a means to support and inspire others around the globe.

As someone who has through sheer grit, determination and resilience, with a huge splattering of female support, not only survived against some hefty odds but she has flipped the trauma into something positive. By unashamedly sharing her journey, not only of abuse within the home but also, institutional abuse that continues to keep women and children in dangerous situations, Sophia aims to secure more protection for the most vulnerable of our communities because she lives by the motto of #strongertogether.

Sophia now works to provide support and safety to those within society who have had a traumatic start in life and helps to guide them to fulfil their potential. She also spends much of her time writing. Her new books are on the horizon and others in the form of newsletters and other publications.

When not working, she can normally be found at the beach taking in the sunset or wandering around the countryside, normally chatting to herself.

(scan the QR code for Sophia's book)

https://www.amazon.co.uk/Escaping-Bohemia-Sophia-Moseley/dp/ B08HBKJXKB/

One Foot Over The Cliff

"I spent a whole month, yes a *whole* month, it was so important that I got it right, trying to work out how I could jump off a cliff, or possibly drive off a cliff at one of my favourite walking spots without my children feeling the pain of a parent committing suicide and the added abandonment. Now, at this precise moment, the thought of this, not only sends a shiver down my spine but makes me giggle and not because I in any way find it funny but in realising how confused my brain was at this time. How lost I was at that moment, albeit extended moment. I guess that I can blame complex PTSD for that, though. Maybe it is a nervous giggle as I was one step away from causing my daughters more pain and trauma than they had previously known and for that I would have had to accept responsibility. I spent every waking moment trying to devise a plan, which is damn right crippling when you are in the clutches of a mental and physical breakdown. The torture didn't stop when my eyes shut though, still my psyche wanted to be released from the pain, shame and torment that hung in my body like Victorian fog over London Bridge.

I spent every moment that I was not on auto pilot, taking my child to school or trying to complete mundane chores in the home, playing out my death in my mind, like a movie. If I did it like this or perhaps like this, maybe my children would be less traumatised or think that I hadn't taken my own life. If I did this, they may think that I had been murder or if I did this, they would think it was just an accident. This, my friends, is what an abused mind looks like. This is the mind of a woman who has nothing left to give, who is at the bottom of 'rock bottom'. *The grit had gone!* Now, in my sound mind-I say sound rather loosely-I feel such pain and empathy for that woman that occupied my body back in 2020. She had been so brave and had managed to ask 'him' to leave but the pain not only continued but intensified. The torment and even the torture continued to slowly suck the life from my every moment.

How did I come to be in this shocking space? I hear you ask and I have asked myself a million times, as I try to rationalise my mind from this period of my life. Yes my husband had left the family home and this time he had stayed gone. In other words I had stayed strong and kept my distance from him. If I am honest and to help to empower others, we have to be truthful with such topics as domestic abuse. I regretted my choice of separation nearly as soon as I had made it. This regret would increase and decrease over the coming years as I pushed forward and struggled to loosen his grip on me and my children. As a note, by the time I am no longer married to this man and all matters have been resolved it will be five years since I asked him to leave and since I have seen him. That's the truth of trying to leave an abuser and how it is made even more difficult than it needs to be. That of course is a totally different story, to be shared at another time.

So back to the question, how, why and what had led to this point of near utter destruction for myself and two exquisite children. When I met this man, I was not looking or longing for a relationship, I didn't yearn to meet my soul mate or find a father for the child from my first marriage. I was happy, settled and excited for a new future that I hadn't actually planned for, but was willing to embrace, with my beautiful little daughter. I had enrolled in some qualifications that I hadn't had the chance to take when I was younger. I studied after work, when my daughter was in bed. We were building an amazing network of friends around us and making plans for our future as she grew up and I just grew. Our future looked bright, drizzled with a little fear. It's scary being solely responsible for another soul and yourself, even as an adult.

Then one evening an old friend invited me out, something that I had not done for over eight years. I accepted albeit a little resistant, as socialising wasn't something that I enjoyed or came easy. However, as another step to me being a fully functional adult, I knew it was time to step out of my comfort zone and as a bonus the evening involved dancing and I love to dance.

Towards the end of my grown up evening which was filled with reminiscing, dancing and laughing until my belly hurt and let's not forget the dreaded 'mummy guilt', my friend and I met a young man, who had a sparkle and quirkiness to him that made me intrigued. He was polite, even though a little drunk, he was a curious creature and just a touch flirtatious, but not enough for it to be an 'ick' moment. It turned out that he lived right by my friend's house, so as the designated driver I offered him a lift, with no intention of it going any further than that. That night the first red flag was thrown in my face but I, a woman with a small child who had had no romantic interaction whatsoever, no compliments, no flirting with the opposite for over eighteen months, closed my eyes as the red flag hit me straight in the forehead. Just before he got out of the car, with my friend sitting in the back, he turned and smiled, his eyes twinkling with the kind of sweet mischief that I thought would be fun, he asked for my number and as I said to myself "What's the worst that could happen," as I thought that this would be just some short term fun and what fully grown woman doesn't want or need a little admiration now and again. I handed over my number. He joyously put this into his Nokia phone and said "I'll text you soon." My friend and I giggled as I felt like a desirable young woman again, not a woman with a small child whose first husband had left her for a younger model.

As we drive down the road, which I soon discover is connected by a walkway from his house to the next street, the phone rings and this manly but excitable voice said "Just checking you had given me the right number", as I looked out of the car window, there stands this young, now eager man waving. He had run down the alley to the next street, just in case I had given him the wrong number. As we both giggle he puts down the phone and waves as we drive away. I turn to my friend and she says "Sweet" and I feel desired and elated. Looking back with twenty years spent with this man and working in the field of domestic abuse for the last three years, it's clear to see that this is a controlling man, who likes to get what he wants and is not afraid to make sure that he does. Which springs this question to my mind, "What would he have done at that moment, if I had given him the wrong number?"

After that first hook, he continued to reel me in like a master fisherman. Within two weeks he told me about his colourful past, he didn't have to at that point but cooed to me "I like you so much and you are so special I feel that I need to tell you the truth." He of course didn't tell me the whole truth and this 'truth' came to bite me in the bum later on, when he would scream in drunken or drug fuelled rages "You knew who I was when you met me." At the time though I thought what an admiral quality to be so honest about choices that he had made in the past. He didn't have to tell me, he only just met me, this wasn't going to be the love affair of the century, so he could have kept his past to himself. I valued that he had trusted me enough to share such personal experiences and believed him wholeheartedly when he said that he had been clean for over a year. I know some would argue that this is not necessarily a red flag but in this situation it was yet again a hook and control tactic that I fell for. Please bear in mind that *I fell for him hook, line and sinker!* I of course didn't share this information with any of my friends, because what type of person would I be to share someone else's personal experiences and let's add a bit of honesty here, I wanted everyone in my life to like him as much as I was beginning to do. What wasn't to like, he was younger than me and handsome-this is a sure ego booster, honest-a massive tick, generous-I only saw him every two weeks so he spoilt me and my daughter for two days and then went back to work and thoughtful, to name just a few 'qualities' that shone through in those first few months. Even though I am sure on his part there was some truth in his 'love bombing' behaviour at the beginning of our journey, looking back I can see it for what it was, another way to entice commitment from me. I had fallen and fallen hard, I thought I was so lucky for another chance. I had started to feel, this man is my soulmate, something that I had never believed in previously, this man was changing my opinion of love and men in general, that can't be a bad thing surely? I could have the family that I have desired from childhood! Couldn't I?

The next six months continued as I became more engrossed in this man and our relationship as he showered me with a kind of love that I had never experienced before, tender, passionate and full of laughter. He knew me, he got me and I felt that I could at last be myself. I shared things that I had never shared, this just reinforced the fact that this was meant to be, my knight in shining armour had arrived and I would live happily ever after. Any hiccups that arose, like girls sending shocking messages, strange interactions between him and his mother, more snippets about past experiences were just overlooked as they were explained away and covered up by more subtle and not so understated gestures, such as when he was working 268 miles away but decided to surprise me on the evening of my birthday with gifts, balloons and a takeaway then proceed to get up at 1am to get back to work on time the next morning. How could this not be the man of my dreams?

After a while I, on my own, bought my first apartment for myself and my daughter and of course he moved in, still working away, so the honeymoon continued cementing my belief and trust in him. I was so happy and positive about our future.

I fell pregnant and we spoke about him finding work close to home once our baby was born and he was excited and thoughtful about the arrival of his first child. He had formed a great relationship with my daughter and they had decided between them that he would become 'dad' so I just knew he was going to be absolutely wonderful with this new little baby. He researched the best pram system, which he chose and bought. He did the same with the new car that we bought in both our names. I was so enthralled that he was so concerned about every aspect of our lives that he took the time to make sure everything was perfect and it took the strain off of me. I felt cared for, protected and I felt that my children and I were safe and always would be. This is all I wanted as a child. At last my childhood dreams had come true so it was easy to let little *mistakes or upsets* go, I mean no one is perfect, are they?

Over the next eighteen years this man slowly but surely destroyed the young women who danced the night away laughing with her friend. He destroyed the woman that he made feel beautiful and desired above all other women. He demolished any self-esteem and value that the women who promised her child a brighter future had. I literally didn't know if I was coming or going, whether it was me or him or I was imagining everything. Of course, at first, it was a slow and gradual process, no daily beatings or drunken rages or being missing for days, this and other kinds of degrading behaviours were sprinkled over periods of love, fun times while building a home and family where we both, along with our children could find the peace that we had been searching for, but previously searching in the wrong places. This my new friends is how women stay in abusive and dangerous situations far longer than seems sane, it's because the abuser is so very apt at making the victim feel insane. And insane I was, insane for staying, insane because half the time I was trying to paper over the cracks that turned into valleys, insane because I questioned how much I was contributing to the problem and pattern and insane because I didn't see my own worth or reach out for help.

With each outburst, problem or abusive moment it got easier to either forgive or forget, as I thought to myself, If I forgave him for that I now have to do it for this, because this is less serious than that was. Please tell me that someone understands that kind of madness. As the years pass it gets even easier for the covert abuser to exhibit their true self more often and openly, as the victim thinks of all the years that they have already invested in, the children, their future and then that mad thought appears. I can wait until the children leave home, then I'll leave. Yep, I thought that, I thought that I could control the situation, and that I could in part control him, just so the children could have a nice and normal childhood. The 2.4 kids, two cars and a dog kind of family, who are always holding hands and smiling at each other and are and always will be madly head over heels in love. Please someone ban Disney movies, I beg of you.

As I write this, my heart goes out to that woman, the me of so many years, the woman who only wanted the simple things in life, love, security and a good family for her children. The woman who cried herself to sleep too many times to remember, who was constantly worried, didn't speak up, avoided him when he was in a mood and inadvertently taught her children the same thing. This woman needed someone to hold her and tell her, *"Babe, this is not right, you are worth so much more and you can choose to do what is right for you."* And I did…eventually!

So that is how I spent a whole month in the later part of 2020 trying to escape the agony that I was surprisingly still feeling after the marriage had ended. I say surprisingly because I naively thought once he left the pain and numbness that I had felt for some many years would go with him, maybe in his heart and body, instead of mine. That didn't happen. The abuse towards me and our family had caused such severe complex PTSD that I didn't know who I was anymore or basically what was day or night.

The day came when I had decided to drive to my favourite walking spot, along a coastal path in the South East of England and just keep on walking off the cliff, instead of following the winding narrow path that runs next to the cliff edge. I had realised that there was no way to make it as easy as I wanted to for my children but the mess in my mind was also not helping them to heal or move on. His parting words just constantly rang in my ears, "You'll never make it without me," and I was ready to succumb to this and allow my children the suffering of seeing me fail at life as well as marriage. Yes, this decision caused me great sadness and thus added to my confused state. As I was about to leave what I hoped would be our forever home, when we bought it twelve years earlier, face puffy from crying for months, hair upkeep, and clothes that could have stood up without my body inside, my phone rang. A close friend was at the other end of the line and though I tried to give the impression of a woman with all her shit together, this empathic friend felt and knew different. She asked to facetime me and instantly saw that I was far from being able to hold a bag of groceries safely let alone the mess of a life, or what I perceived was a mess. As the conversation progressed I trusted her with my true feelings and intentions. She asked me to promise to just stay safe and not do anything at all until she had spoken to another close friend of hers, who happened to be a counsellor. I promised her but in my heart I knew that I was lying, I couldn't live with this torment any longer. Drained from the honesty of the call I decided to go back to bed. This was a normal place to take refuge under the safety of my quilt.

Luckily I never got a chance to fulfil the plan of taking a long walk and not coming back as later that evening I received a call from my friend's counsellor friend and even though I find it hard to talk to anyone let alone strangers, my healing began there with this amazing woman, who has now become one of my best friends. I was blessed that she said that she wouldn't charge me but asked that when I felt stronger would I do her business photography, as this was a passion of mine. She offered to support me as and when I needed her, at first this was a couple of sessions a week and then as time went by these decreased. It wasn't plain sailing by any stretch of the imagination, it was two steps forward and seventy back, straight back into hell. Now, I know that healing isn't meant to be easy but it sure is worth it.

Now four years on, still trying to divorce him and settle the financial matters, see how the controller still tries to control, I am living my life, my way. I don't fear a Friday evening anymore, trying to anticipate his mood. I don't try to manage everyones moods and feelings to avoid an outburst, instead I manage my moods. Yes some things are still difficult, infuriating and draining-particularly the system that allows this continued control, but each day is a blessing, time with my most breathtaking daughters is worth every ounce of pain that I felt in those early days. When they say "Mum, we are so much happier and at peace now," I know that I now have the family that I always dreamt of. How truly blessed am I to receive this type of gift. Just because I, with the help and support of some astounding women around me, believed it could and would get better.

Now this is just a snippet of the story within an abusive relationship, the pain and uphill struggle once I decided I could no longer allow his toxic behaviour and personality around my two beautiful daughters, who deserved to see and be around the best version of a man, not something from a horror documentary. There obviously is so much more detail and moments that caused torture to the souls of my children and my own soul and one day I will share the whole story. However, by giving a little glimpse into my story I hope that it shows even when you have one foot over the cliff edge there is still hope and there is always something wonderful to hold onto, life will not only get better but you will feel freedom like never before.

As I tap away on my keyboard, allowing some of these excruciating memories to climb out of the box in the back of my mind and ease out onto the screen I realise with gladness how far I have come, even while still in the last lap of the race. By sharing my journey so far over the last few years, as I ceased to hold any of the blame and let the shame dissipate I have realised that I am not alone, many women have travelled this path or one very alike and it seems that we all have one similar contributing factor to our survival and success, that is the support of other strong women who are unafraid to walk the dark path with us, offering comfort, help and honesty, in equal measure. We don't need or expect someone to fix our problems but *someone to sit in the darkness with us until we see the sun rise again.*

This brings me to the ladies, girls and children who still fear Friday nights, a drunk father or a man who manipulates people and situations just to make himself more of a man than he is. Domestic abuse is for the most part a hidden crime, until a victim feels strong enough to share what is happening to them, when they reach out for help or until authorities are involved, potentially when there is a death. Though it is impossible to number how many are suffering domestic abuse, The Crime Survey in England and Wales, March 2023, found that one in four women have suffered domestic abuse since the age of sixteen.

To those women who sit alone and think of negative or drastic ways in which they and their children can escape their tormentor please reach out, reach out to someone who you can trust and who will hold your hand while you find the strength that you need to travel this path. Reach out to charities and organisations that can give you empathy, practical support along with a belief in you which they can help you see and feel. I feel blessed to have found Hopefull Handbags when I did because this charity helped me find my wings…then there was no stopping me.

To all I would say trust your instincts, we are divine beings who have all the knowledge we need within ourselves. If our gut is telling us something is wrong, then it is wrong, so listen and act. If my friend had not called me back in 2020 I would not be here, if my counsellor had not believed that I would heal and be able to provide the best business portraiture for her (though I think she would have been there for me without this trade exchange) my children would be preparing for their fifth Christmas without me and no doubt without a family home and if I hadn't held onto the little flicker of light deep inside my gut, giving me hope, I would not be looking forward to all the adventures that await me.

We have these experiences, not because we deserve them or cause them, that blame lays firmly at the door of someone else-the abuser, but maybe so we can assist others once or even while we heal.

"The trauma we carry is not our fault but our healing is our responsibility."

This chapter is dedicated to the strongest and most loyal women I know, my daughters. Thank you for standing by me, holding me up and supporting me all the way. Without you both, I would have not made it through the dark nights. Here's to many more years together filled with laughter and mischief. I will always love you both, more than I could ever say or show you.

Love Mummy xxx

KERRIE HAVERN

Kerrie Havern, is a former wedding and event planner, boxing coach, charity founder, community activist and is a single mum to Finn.

Kerrie, from Newry, County Down, is extremely passionate about people and community, this is evident in the extensive charity work she does as an individual as well as the cofounder of Caring Coins Association, a community based café and charity. The tag line is Our Community, Our Responsibility. Kerrie and her trustees are passionate about ensuring all members and segments of the community have a safe space, a supportive environment and system to allow them to live a happier healthier life. The focus is on supporting physical and mental health through a warm, safe space to come and have a cuppa and a chat or via the many weekly events and groups ranging from crafting, to wellness, the busy bees and SEND community gatherings as well as educational talks.

Kerrie is also a proud Strikeback Self Defence Instructor supporting women and children through self defence workshops and empowering others to use their voice, boundaries and simple techniques to stay safe.

(scan the QR code to visit Kerrie Havern's website)

https://linktr.ee/KerrieHavern

Thriving Not Surviving

"Be kind, take care, spread love."
– Kerrie Havern

"I miss you, the kids miss you, my mum is asking for you, I love you, I had a holiday booked for us, you need me, I'll go to counselling, I'll quit drinking, I bought us a kayak."

These were the words that were repeated to me over and over again and formed the many reasons why I kept taking him back to the point I stopped seeing friends and family because I was embarrassed to tell anyone. My mental health was being damaged. My confidence was non-existent to the point it felt as if my soul was being destroyed.

A few years prior, we met on a night out. I recognised him as our paths had crossed previously. He ticked all the boxes, handsome, owned his own business and was a fellow single parent. I had been single for years and was holding out for "the one", and I thought it was going to be him. It was perfect on the surface.

At the time, I was a boxing coach and was well respected in my club and was part of a brilliant team. We ran charity white-collar events to help raise money for local charities. I loved volunteering as a coach at the club and ran the children's classes and private sessions for couples. He had been a boxer when he was younger and agreed to sign up for our white-collar boxing tournament that we were running that coming November. I was so chuffed, as I was the lead coach for training and we would get to train together. He enjoyed cycling, running and the outdoors all things I looked forward to doing together.

The first of many red flags happened but I ignored it, he would arrive at the club when I was training one-on-one with a male client and say he was just passing, then kiss me in front of my client and leave. It was as if he was marking his territory.

I let it go. I thought it was coming from a place of insecurity. I was volunteering in a male-dominated environment and didn't think anything more of it.

When we went out for a night, everyone would comment, on how well we were suited and how "I" was good for him. No one ever commented that he was good for me, another ignored red flag.

I began to notice that I hadn't seen any of my friends in a while, we would message each other and if I mentioned going out with the girls, he would already have plans for us. At first, I thought it was so nice but then I organised to go for dinner with my girlfriends and his behaviour became somewhat passive-aggressive by saying "Oh, so I'm not invited?!" Eventually, I didn't go.

This was the first of many times I felt he was trying to put me in my place. I was supposed to have gone out with my girlfriends, but to keep the peace, I cancelled and told them I couldn't get a babysitter. I agreed to cook for us and he was happy again. He didn't turn up at 6 pm as planned, he didn't arrive until almost 11 pm and had had more than enough to drink, telling me stories of having to meet his landlord and having to have a pint with him. This became a regular occurrence on Friday evenings and after a while, I got sick of it all.

I attempted to break up with him after 3 months together. This would prove the first of many attempts. It was 2 weeks before a big club boxing event. He was absent from training and plans we made together during the lead-up to this event. I felt like a puppet, with him pulling all the strings. I was adamant that this was not good for me or my son, so I sent him a message saying it was over.

The phone started with calls and messages, with "sorry" and "I love you" and the messages did not stop. This continued relentlessly. He arrived at my house, declaring his love and how we were so good for each other and he would not mess up again. With the pressure I was already under getting everything ready for fight night, I caved in. This was one less fight for me to have to engage in.

I told him it was over about 10 times over 3 years. Each time he would guilt and bombard me with texts and missed calls, making me feel worn down until I took him back.

When I asked if he wanted to make plans for the weekend, he implied I was controlling and trying to control him. In my head, my mind was roaring at me, "It's normal to make plans with your partner", but his voice was louder. And each time I took him back, he would treat me like a queen and then the cycle would start again.

Within a week, all promises made were out the window. On one occasion, it barely lasted a day. He had taken me to one of my favourite restaurants, I had bought a new dress and I felt good about myself. As soon as we went in, it went wrong!

A man we both knew was serving in the restaurant, I gave him a hug and both men shook hands and we went to our table. As we waited for our starters, I could feel his frustration and asked if anything was wrong. "No!" he retorted and said he was going for a cigarette. I sat waiting for him and after about 20 minutes, I went to the bathroom and then outside for a cigarette.

He wasn't in the smoking area when I arrived. I decided that if he was in a bad mood, I would give him space. I took my time having a cigarette and chatting to others in the smoking area.

When I went back in, he was like a spitting demon, demanding to know where I had been. I couldn't understand his anger. I asked politely where he thought I had been. He immediately snapped, "For all I know, you were out the back having sex with the waiter over the kegs". I couldn't believe such a feral, toxic accusation and burst into tears.

How could he think I would do something so despicable? By the end of the meal, I just wanted to go home alone, but he clearly felt like he had apologised enough and everything was fine again. It was not.

The relationship was toxic, if anything went wrong in his day, he drowned his sorrows and frustration at the nearest bar, regardless of our plans. I felt so depressed, that I took refuge in my bed. From the time my son was collected for school and came home, I stayed in bed. It felt like he had drained the life right out of me. I'd break up with him and he would hound me until I gave in, and only because I had nothing to fight him with.

I realised in the summer of lockdown 2020, that I had to get out of the relationship for good and regardless of how attached I was to his children. My child was my responsibility and I didn't want him growing up in the environment we felt stuck in.

That was it, I deserved better, and my son deserved a happy and healthy mother. As soon as my son left for the West of Ireland to spend time with his father, I called time on the relationship again.

This time was different. I rallied my girlfriends and told them everything. They were so supportive, and I needed them more than I realised. The barrage of messages began again; text messages, WhatsApp, Snapchat, Facebook Messenger, the list went on and on.

I blocked him on all social media channels and blocked his phone number. This did not stop his tsunami of phone calls from withheld numbers, 20 of them in 9 minutes. I answered one call to tell him to stop. The relationship was over.

He replied that if I didn't speak to him he would arrive at my house and make me talk to him. I immediately turned to my dad and step-mum and told them what had been happening. For the duration I was in their house, I had a further 11 missed calls. The next time the phone rang, my step-mum took the phone and told him, "That's enough now! She doesn't want to go out with you, it's over. Now leave her alone because I will not hesitate to call the police. This has on gone long enough, goodbye."

It didn't stop him, he banged my door, driving dangerously in and out of the estate which caused a neighbour to reach out and check on my well-being. The situation was spiralling out of control, 154 missed calls in one day alone. I asked my cousin to ask him to stop. The relationship had become toxic and it was over.

I asked my cousin to keep it pleasant, which he promised to do.

As soon as my cousin left, half an hour later he was sitting back in my kitchen, telling me he told my cousin that, I had a drink problem and not to pay any attention to what I was saying. We would be back together by the following week or as soon as I saw sense. I couldn't believe what he was saying to me and I broke down in tears.

My mind felt so confused. I went through all the breakups and all the times I tried to do it politely, compassionately and clearly. I avoided hurtful comments. I felt I had tried everything, apart from being nasty. I unblocked his number and sent him a message, calling him everything you can imagine, telling him I didn't love him and never wanted to see him again. In my head, it was clear and direct. How wrong was I! His instant reply was "You wouldn't say those things if you didn't love me." I couldn't believe his response when I specifically said "I do not want to see you, I do not love you". He interpreted this incorrectly. I had to block him again.

In the following days, the constant withheld phone calls came flooding in followed by voicemails. In one voicemail he promised to leave me alone if I would just meet him to talk. During these 6 weeks, my friends were by my side giving me the strength to hold my course and get him out of my life. I told my best friend about the voicemail and we talked about the possibility of me saying it was over straight to his face.

Perhaps if I stared him in the face, with no love in my eyes, he would finally move on and leave me in peace. I agreed to meet him in a busy car park and my friend came with me. As soon as I arrived, he commented on my friend driving me to meet him, as if I wasn't safe. We spoke in his van. At that moment I was brave and told him I wasn't afraid and that this was over. It was a toxic cycle, I was breaking up directly with him and reminded him he had promised to leave me be.

As I went to jump out of his van, he told me he had been enquiring about renting a house for us. My immediate reaction and reply was that we had broken up 6 weeks ago and I would not be moving anywhere. I refused to feel caged any longer. I hopped out of the van and once again, told him it was over. His chilling response was "No it's not".

Shaking like a leaf with adrenaline, I got back into my friend's car and told her everything. She was as bewildered as I was.

We went to her house for tea and spoke with her husband. The situation dumbfounded him. The phone calls didn't stop but I stopped listening to the voicemails, at least I had control over that. After another week of numerous calls from withheld numbers, I unblocked him again. I begged him to stop, reminding him that the relationship was over and I was never returning.

His reply sent chills through my whole body, he said, "It is women like you that make men commit suicide". I felt sick, how could he say something like that to me or about me?

I rang my cousin who I had always been close to growing up. She arrived on my doorstep 20 minutes later with a friend and my sister. I needed all the support I could get. My cousin was furious, as were the others and she made the decision I did not feel brave to make.

She rang the police and told them about the messages and outlined the situation. The constable asked to speak to me and with the support of the women around me, I started to confide in the constable. She was so gentle and empathetic.

I told her about the missed calls. I told her I had received 24 calls in 11 minutes and over 100 calls in one day. Her tone instantly changed, still kind but official, "I'm going to have one of my colleagues call you on this number in the next half hour, we will get this sorted".

I hung up and felt so confused. The realisation of it all hit me, I was a victim. Within half an hour, a second constable rang and again she was kind but authoritarian. She told me that she had read the transcript and was aware of my situation and that she and her male colleague would be handling things from this point onwards. She told me that they would be calling to his house to instruct him to cease all contact with me and they would ring me when this action was carried out. They were taking this seriously.

She rang again that evening to say she had been and told him the relationship was over and if he did not leave alone, she would be back and would be using the full power of the laws on domestic violence to make her arrest. She asked about my son. I told her he was in the West of Ireland, safe with his father and was due back that coming Friday. She advised me to contact my son's father and ask him to let my son stay for another week. She also suggested I stay somewhere else for a few days.

I asked my mummy to ring my son's father. I couldn't face having to tell him this had happened. At the moment, I blamed myself for letting it happen and for letting it continue for almost 3 years. I felt so angry and ashamed.

How could I let myself be walked over like that?

My son's father was very supportive and was delighted with the extra time. I contacted an old friend who lived a couple of towns away. I explained the situation and he invited me to stay and chill out for a few days. The following week, I had no calls from a withheld number and felt I was able to breathe. The constable rang me that week to do a wellness check and ask if I had heard from him. I was happy I hadn't and thanked her and her colleagues for their help.

After that, he followed me through my village twice but only on one occasion tried to speak to me, I told him "no", but as soon as he approached me, he went away. I didn't hear from him again.

I suspect he may have found a new focus for his attention and distorted affections.

By the summer of 2020, although in lockdown, I was finally free from him but my mental health didn't bounce back so quickly. My best friend was also struggling with her mental health after the sudden and tragic death of her mother and brother and in April 2020, we started fundraising.

During this time, we relied heavily on each other and decided to focus on something positive to distract us. At this time many people were fundraising for the National Health Service. We set up a Facebook page called "Caring Coins" using all the coins we collected to care for the National Health Service workers. We put a big container at my door and encouraged people to call past on their daily drive and drop off jars of spare change and coins.

The first day that people started calling with their loose change, was the first day we started to feel a slight lift. Over the following month, we ran our first appeal. People were calling from all over the area but rather than just drop their change in the container and leave, they were keeping a safe distance and talking to us. One woman stood for almost an hour speaking to us as we were the first people she'd spoken to in 6 weeks. At that point, we realised as much as focusing on the appeal was lifting us, it was also lifting the people who were donating.

A new journey had started, it was full of love and kindness and was helping me thrive and to find myself again. We were put back into lockdown that winter again and we heard of families facing struggles over Christmas. We went to a local hardware store and bought orange builders containers and started going door to door, asking people for their loose change. Other people got in touch who wanted to come and help us and some days there were 15 - 20 volunteers collecting change.

We raised over £23,000 and helped over 500 families in our local area for Christmas that first year. At a time when the world stood still, we stood up.

Caring Coins Association is in its third year as a registered charity in Northern Ireland and has been running for 5 years. We opened our first community café in 2023. The cafe is a safe warm space for anyone who may feel a little isolated to call in for tea, coffee and a chat. We also run events for single parents, self-care days, offer advice, run ladies' nights and bingo, to name a few. This journey has opened many doors for me and reaffirmed my self-worth to myself and with the women who have helped me along the way.

My journey is only beginning and has given me peace in my life again.

Since we started Caring Coins, I have trained in
- Conflict mediation
- Walk leadership
- Take5 ambassador
- Community health training

I am the first Certified Strike Back Self Defence © female self-defence instructor in Northern Ireland.

All of these tools along with my own experiences, have guided me to where I believe I am supposed to be; helping other women, giving them the support they need to become strong again and I cannot wait to get started.

The last 4 years have taught me there is so much strength when we support each other.

My final words are:
- Trust your gut
- A red flag is a red flag
- You can find yourself again and come back even stronger
- Don't be afraid to ask for help, you are not alone.

This chapter is dedicated to my son, Finn, who makes my heart smile every day.

SUZANNE GOLDSTEIN

Suzanne Goldstein is a health and wellness advocate and dedicated supporter of women's empowerment. She is a loving mother to her beautiful daughter and a proud cat mom.

Suzanne Goldstein, from the United States, is deeply committed to holistic health and wellness, a passion she explores through spending time at the beach, practicing yoga, journaling, spirituality, and meditation. Her love for a balanced lifestyle also extends to discovering and sharing healthy tips that inspire others to live well.

As a survivor of a 20-year abusive marriage, she understands firsthand the challenges women face in breaking free and rebuilding their lives. Her mission is to serve women and their children who are experiencing abuse, offering hope, resources, and a path to serenity and abundance on their own terms. She believes every woman deserves a peaceful, fulfilling life, and she is dedicated to empowering them to realize their worth.

Suzanne actively supports this mission through Hopefull Handbags Global nonprofit and is on the Board of Directors, providing safe spaces, resources, and guidance for women and their children in need. She takes pride in turning her challenges into opportunities to uplift others, always striving to see the good in every situation and extend her support where it is needed most. Her ultimate goal is to help as many women as possible reclaim their lives and embrace their true potential.

In her free time, she enjoys spending time with her daughter, going to the beach, refinishing furniture, using her creativity to design inspiring pieces for her home, and snuggling with her cat.

(scan the QR code to visit Suzanne Goldstein's website)

https://zzatem.com/SuzanneGoldstein

Breaking Free, My Journey Through Abuse to Resilience

"Let Go of What Was, Accept What Is, Have Faith in What Will Be."
— Sonia Ricotti

It All Started When I Fell in Love with a Narcissistic Abuser

At 26, I was swept off my feet by a man who seemed to embody everything I had ever wanted: charm, humor, stability, and love. I was drawn to him like a moth to a flame, captivated by his magnetic presence and the way his laughter filled the room like the comforting crackle of a fire on a cold night. I didn't stop to question whether the light was real or just a fire waiting to consume me. I thought I had finally found my forever love.

Looking back now, I can see with stark clarity that I didn't know my worth. If I had, I wouldn't have ignored the red flags or silenced the nagging gut feelings that whispered warnings like a faint echo in a cavern. But I was young, searching for connection, stability, and validation, things I had never fully received growing up. Raised in a fractured home with a mother battling mental illness and a father who was emotionally distant, I craved love and acceptance. When this man swept into my life with all the right words and gestures, I clung to the idea that he might be my safe haven.

The truth, however, couldn't have been further from that fantasy. What started as a fairytale romance soon unraveled into a nightmare, a nightmare that would hold me captive for over 23 years.

The Illusion of Love

In the beginning, he seemed perfect. He was attentive, funny, and kind. His gaze felt like sunlight breaking through storm clouds, making me feel chosen, seen, and valued in ways I had never experienced. But narcissistic abuse often begins this way, with a facade so convincing that even the most intuitive among us can't see through it. He was playing a role, and I was one of the characters in his carefully crafted play. All of it was a lie. Every word, every gesture, every kiss, every touch.

Our dating relationship was rocky, marked by periods of intense connection and abrupt disconnection. He would discard me, then come back, claiming he couldn't live without me. I mistook this cycle of behavior for love, and

I kept going back. Each time, I believed his promises that things would be different. Each time, I was wrong.

When he finally proposed, I felt like I had won some grand prize. He chose me. That act alone seemed to validate my worth, a dangerous and flawed perception that would take me years to unlearn. Looking back, I see now that his proposal wasn't about love or commitment; it was about control. He knew I was close to walking away for good, and he needed a way to secure his grip on me and I fell for it.

The Subtle Erosion of Self

Once we were married, the cracks in his facade began to show. His temper, which had been present during our dating years, became more pronounced. I believe I ignored the warning signs in our dating relationship, likely because his anger was never directed at me, making it easier to rationalize or dismiss his behavior. However, now his criticisms landed like stones, each one chipping away at my confidence. He was critical of everything: my cooking, my parenting, even the way I spoke. At first, I tried harder to please him, thinking if I just did things his way, then he would be happy. But nothing was ever enough. It was never-ending.

One of the hardest parts of living with a narcissistic abuser is the slow erosion of self. It doesn't happen all at once. Instead, it's a steady chipping away at your confidence, your autonomy, and your sense of reality. Over time, I began to doubt myself. Was I really a bad cook? Was I too sensitive? Was I the reason he was always angry?

I didn't realize it then, but I was being psychologically abused. His criticisms, his outbursts, and his constant need to control every aspect of our lives were all forms of abuse. But because he wasn't physically abusive, at least not at first, I told myself it wasn't that bad.

I often felt like I was walking on eggshells. The air in our home was thick with tension as if it were holding its breath, waiting for the next outburst. Even the smallest things, a glass not clean enough to his liking, or spilled water on the counter, could ignite his fury. It was like living in the shadow of an unpredictable storm, always bracing for the next lightning strike.

Becoming a Mother

When our daughter was born, everything changed. She became my everything. Her tiny fingers wrapping around mine felt like a lifeline, tethering me to hope. I poured all my love, energy, and hope into her, determined to give her the stability and affection I had longed for as a child. But even she wasn't safe from his anger.

One night, when she was just four months old, she started crying in her bassinet. Exhausted, I hoped he would get up and take care of her. Instead, he reached over me and hit the bassinet three times, yelling at her to be quiet. My heart shattered like glass hitting a cold, hard floor. I got up immediately, holding her close, and told him never to do that again.

That moment was a turning point. From then on, I became fiercely protective of my daughter, shielding her from his temper as best I could. Over the years, he directed his anger at her in small but significant ways. An arm smacked, a harsh word spoken in frustration. But I stood my ground, making it clear that I would not tolerate him hurting her.

The sound of her laughter became my solace, a reminder that there was still light in our lives. I would hold her close, breathing in her baby-soft scent, vowing silently to protect her at all costs. Her giggles, her tiny footsteps walking towards me, her joyful squeals as we played together, these moments kept me going.

The Weight of Control

As the years went on, his need for control became more apparent. He discouraged me from working full-time, knowing that financial independence would give me the freedom to leave. Instead, I stayed home, raising our daughter, managing both our businesses from home, and taking care of our household. While I was grateful for the time with my daughter, there was a price to pay. I became isolated, financially dependent, and increasingly trapped. Slowly but surely, he chipped away at my sense of autonomy until I hardly recognized myself.

The walls of our home felt like a prison. Even the sunshine streaming through the windows seemed muted, unable to penetrate the gloom that hung over us. My days were filled with routines that revolved around his needs, making sure his dinners were prepared, even though he was never happy with just about anything I prepared, ensuring the house was tidy, and tiptoeing around his moods.

The First Strike

The first time he hit me, it was with a spatula. We had been married for over 17 years by then, and I was stunned. The sting of it lingered, not just on my skin but deep within me. He didn't apologize, didn't even acknowledge what he had done. He just stared at me with a blank expression that chilled me to the core.

I told myself it was a one time thing, an anomaly in an otherwise difficult but manageable marriage. I convinced myself to move on, hoping things would get better. But deep down, I knew something had shifted. We were about a month away from moving to Florida, USA. I felt trapped as I was not on speaking terms with my family and didn't have any close friends.

A New Low

After 17 years of marriage, we moved to Florida, USA, hoping for a fresh start. But the move only amplified his anger and insecurity. He was more volatile than ever, and his moods became impossible to predict.

The second time he hit me, two years after the first, it was like a monster had erupted from within him. His rage was no longer just a simmering threat. It was a tangible force that I could no longer ignore. By then, I was already planning my escape, but his physical abuse added urgency to my efforts.

The Breaking Point

In the autumn of 2021, our daughter ended up in the hospital, overwhelmed by anxiety. My heart was breaking. Watching her struggle was unbearable. I felt like I had failed her. I hadn't protected her enough from the toxicity of our home.

Not long after, she told me that she felt her father was holding me back. Her words were a mirror, reflecting the truth I had been too afraid to face. I knew then that I couldn't stay any longer, not for me, but for her.

Finding Hope

In my despair, I found an unexpected lifeline. Through a series of chance encounters, I connected with Cathlene, the CEO of Hopefull Handbags Global. Her organization helps women and children escape domestic abuse, providing them with the tools and resources they need to rebuild their lives.

Cathlene became my angel, guiding me through the process of leaving and offering me a level of support I hadn't known existed. With her help, I began to see a way out, a path to freedom, and a new life for my daughter and me.

Her words were like a lighthouse in a turbulent sea, guiding me safely to shore. The care packages, the late-night phone calls, and the unwavering belief she had in my ability to rebuild my life were lifelines that I clung to as I began to piece my world back together.

The Day I Left

July 26, 2022, was the hardest and most liberating day of my life. That morning, I thought I was just going to look at a room I planned to rent. By the end of the day, I had left my home, my marriage, and the life I had known for over two decades.

My ex-husband's suspicions had been building for weeks. He had gone through my purse, my vehicle, and our closet, piecing together the signs that I was preparing to leave. When he confronted me, his anger was palpable, a thick tension that made the air feel heavy. For the first time in years, I didn't back down. I told him the truth: I was leaving.

My ex-husband was so enraged. He knew he was losing control over me. I reached out to Cathlene. She said it was time to go. So I gathered my things and walked out the door. I didn't know what the future held, but I knew I couldn't stay.

Rebuilding

The months since I left have been a journey of healing and growth. My daughter and I are learning to navigate life on our own, free from the fear and control that once defined our days.

I have had to completely rebuild my life. I was a stay-at-home mom for close to 19 years. The scent of fresh coffee in the mornings, the feel of a pen gliding across my journal, and the sunlight streaming through our new home's windows became small but powerful reminders of my strength.

There are still challenges, of course. Healing is not a linear process, and there are days when the weight of the past feels overwhelming. But there are also moments of joy, moments when I see my daughter smile, moments when I feel a sense of peace I never thought possible.

Building a New Life

Leaving wasn't the end, it was the beginning. My daughter and I have built a life of our own, a life filled with peace, joy, and mutual respect. The lessons we learned in the shadows of abuse have become the foundation of our strength.

Through therapy, introspection, new friendships, and spirituality, we've healed together. I've rediscovered my passion for health and wellness, pursuing a career that fulfills me and provides for us. My daughter, now a young woman, has grown into an independent, resilient individual who inspires me every day.

Together, we've created a fulfilling and successful life. We've turned the pain of the past into purpose, finding hope and light in places we never imagined. Our story is one of resilience, transformation, and the unyielding power of love, the kind of love that starts from within.

Looking Back

Looking back on my childhood, I realize that I had to grow up fast. My mother suffered from mental illness and, in my opinion, displayed narcissistic traits. I often felt the weight of responsibility for taking care of her, my younger brother, and myself. My father, though he loved me very much, a fact I only fully realized after his sudden passing, showed little affection and had a somewhat of a temper. My parents split up when I was eight, and from that point on, life felt unstable and chaotic. However, I didn't feel stable with my parents when they were together. I felt a different kind of instability and chaos with just my mother. I never felt safe or at peace as a young girl.

We moved around frequently, and I attended seven different elementary schools. There was no consistency in my life, no anchor to provide security. My mother favored my younger brother and was distant and hard on me. She seemed angry at me, and I craved her love and connection, but it never came. I grew up longing for love, but I had no real understanding of what it was. This lack of a solid foundation shaped my misguided ideas about love as I got older.

As a young woman, I began searching for the love and safety I never had as a child. I was independent and liked it that way, but I also dreamed of creating my own family, something stable and loving, unlike what I had experienced. At 16, I entered my first relationship with a man over seven years older than me. He was an alcoholic, a drug addict, and abusive. Despite the chaos, I mistook his possessiveness and words for love because I had no healthy models to guide me. The relationship was tumultuous and frightening at times. I had a very scary experience with him when he tried to run me off the road. He was jealous, controlling, and even dangerous, yet I thought I loved him.

Looking back, I understand that I was too young and inexperienced to navigate such a relationship, especially with someone much older who brought so much baggage. My mother didn't seem to notice or take much interest in my life; I often snuck out to see him. Her self-absorption left me feeling even more alone, and to this day, our relationship is distant and strained. We don't speak anymore.

My childhood experiences taught me to equate love with safety and happiness, but this belief led to more pain. When I met my ex-husband, I thought I had finally found someone who would protect me. He made me feel safe at first, but it was a facade to draw me in. Despite the challenges in our marriage, I stayed for 23 years, believing that love and family were the answers to the emptiness I felt inside. I now see how those years shaped me, not as losses but as life lessons.

The most precious gift from that chapter of my life is my daughter. She is my everything and a constant reminder of the love and purpose I sought for so long. Through her, I have found a deeper sense of love and connection than I ever thought possible.

Today, I understand that happiness and self-worth come from within. I've worked hard to rebuild my sense of self, learning to love and value who I am. While the road has been long and filled with pain, I've come to see my past not as a burden but as a teacher. My journey has made me stronger, more compassionate, and more determined to create the life I deserve. I hold hope that one day I will find true love, a love built on mutual respect, kindness, and understanding. Until then, I will continue to nurture the most important relationship of all: the one I have with myself.

Speaking to My Younger Self

If I could go back, I would tell my younger self to stay true to who you are. Don't settle for less than you deserve and never, ever let someone else define your self-worth based on how they feel about you or treat you.

You are worthy on your own.

You are enough, exactly as you are.

Stay aware and alert to any red flags and listen to your intuition. It will lead you. That nagging feeling is your gut telling you what you need, listen carefully.

This chapter is dedicated to my beautiful daughter, my greatest source of strength and inspiration. Through the hardest times in my life, she has been my unwavering support, my reason to keep going, and the light that guides me. Her laughter is like a melody that lifts my spirit, and her resilience pushes me to see the brighter side of every situation.

I am endlessly proud to be her mom. She is my world, my shining star, and my sunshine. Her boundless energy and optimism inspire me daily, and I strive to view life with the same joy and courage she does. She will never fully know how much I appreciate her and all that she has brought into my life.

Watching her grow into an extraordinary young woman and a source of inspiration to others fills my heart with pride. My hope for her is that she always knows she is enough, exactly as she is. My life is infinitely brighter with her in it, and for that, I am forever grateful.

Acknowledgements

This book is more than just a collection of stories of 12 incredible women, but it is a testament to the power of hope transformed into action. It is for every woman who has ever longed for more, not just wishing for change but actively stepping forward to create happiness and a life that aligns with her true self. In fact, it is for any individual, regardless of gender.

We extend our deepest gratitude to the incredible women who have shared their journeys within these pages, for some it was their first foray into sharing their stories and in a written form too! For some, they are more accustomed to sharing but have never collaborated on a book before. To all of you, your patience, dedication, and courage in putting your stories into words have shaped this book into something truly meaningful. As our first collaborative book project, this has been a learning experience for all of us, and we are immensely grateful for the trust you placed in this vision and your patience as we navigated the process and learned alongside you.

A heartfelt thank you to **Aoife Gaffney**, whose dedication and expertise as our editor carried this book through its many stages, a truly enormous task for one person alone. To **Cathlene Miner, CEO of Hopefull Handbags Global Non-Profit**, for believing in this project and allowing us the opportunity to create something tangible that could offer supporters a meaningful way to contribute to this vital cause. To **Orla Kelly**, whose publishing expertise and guidance have been invaluable, and to **Claire Clarke and her cover design team**, who have brought the visual identity of this book to life, we thank you. They say it takes a village to raise a child and it has certainly taken a village of women to get this book to where it is now and it is so befitting and reflective of our tag line We Are Stronger Together.

We also want to acknowledge the unwavering support of our amazing community of **cheerleaders, volunteers, and champions across the world**, whose energy and passion continue to fuel this movement. This book exists because of all of you. It exists for you too.

And finally, to **you, the reader**, thank you for picking up this book, for investing in these stories, and for being part of something greater. May it serve as a reminder that hope is just the beginning. It is the action we take with that hope that creates real, lasting change.

If this book inspires you, we invite you to continue the journey with us- supporting, sharing, and stepping forward into the life you deserve.

Le grá,

Aisling Owens Nash
Hopefull Handbags Global Ireland

If you have been affected by any of the issues raised here, reach out for help.

Hopefull Handbags
https://www.hopefullhandbags.org/

A list of other resources are provided overleaf.

Ulster
Antrim
Women's Aid ABCLN 028 25 632136 or in an emergency always call 999.
Email: admin@womensaidabcln.org
https://womens-aid.org.uk/

Armagh
https://womensaidarmaghdown.org/get-help/help-for-women/
0808 802 1414

Cavan
https://www.womensaid.ie/get-help/support-services/find-support-locally/cavan/
DVAS
Tel: (071) 914 1515
Email: support@dvas.ie
Website: www.domesticviolence.ie

Derry
C/o Foyle Family Justice Centre
7-9 Bishop Street
Derry
BT48 6PL
(028) 7141 6800
info@foylewomensaid.org
www.foylewomensaid.org

Donegal
1800 262677 (Freephone) or (074) 912 6267
ddvsrefuge@gmail.com
www.donegaldomesticviolenceservice.ie

Down
North Down & Ards Women's Aid
Tel: 028 9127 3196
Email: info@ndawomensaid.org

Fermanagh
Fermanagh Women's Aid
Tel: 028 6632 8898
Email: womensaidfermanagh@btopenworld.com
fermanaghwomensaid.com

Monaghan
Tearmann
The Primary Care Building, Roosky, Monaghan
(047) 72311

Tyrone
WDVP
24hr Domestic Violence Freephone Helpline
0800 9171414

Munster
Clare
Clare Haven
Abbey Lodge, Limerick Road Ennis,
Co. Clare. V95 KR72
Email: clientcare@clarehaven.ie
(0)65 6842646
24h: +353 (0)65 6822435
www.clarehaven.ie

Cork
Womens Aid Cork
Helpline Number
021-4277698
Helpline Opening Hours
24 hours, 7 days per week
Cuanlee Refuge Kyrls Quay Cork City T12 HK74
Email: info@cuanleerefuge.org
Website: www.cuanleerefuge.org/

Mná Feasa (Wise women)
021-4211757
mnafeasa@gmail.com
Mon to Fri : 10:00AM to 4:00PM

Kerry
Adapt
ADAPT Women's Refuge
Killeen Road, Tralee,
Co. Kerry
066 7129100
generalmanager@kerryrefuge.com

Limerick
Adapt
ADAPT House
Rosbrien
Limerick
061 412354
1 800 200504
info@adaptservices.ie
www.adaptservices.ie/

Tipperary
Ascend
0505-23999
ascend@ntdc.ie

Cuan Saor (Safe Harbour)
Helpline Number
1800 57 67 57
Helpline Opening Hours 24 hours, 7 days a week
7 Parnell Street
Raheen
Clonmel
Co. Tipperary
E91 VN26
support@cuansaor.org
https://cuansaor.org/

Waterford
Oasis
(051) 370 367
Freephone: 0818 272 372
projectworker@oasishouse.ie

Leinster
Carlow
Carlow Women's Aid
1800 444 944
info@carlowwomensaid.ie
www.carlowwomensaid.ie

Kilkenny
Amber Refuge
Amber Womens Refuge CLG
Lacken
Dublin Road
Kilkenny
R95 NY04
0818 42 42 44
info@amberwomensrefuge.ie

Dublin
Sonas
Helpline Number
1800 222 223
Helpline Opening Hours
24 hours, 7 days a week
info@sonasdomesticabuse.ie
https://www.domesticabuse.ie/
Saoirse (Freedom)
24/7 Helpline
1800 911 221
helpline@sdvs.ie
014630400
Monday – Friday: 9am -5pm
admin@sdvs.ie
Saoirse Housing Association CLG
PO Box 10819
Tallaght
Dublin 24
Outreach & Court Accompaniment
087-1049863
outreach@sdvs.ie
Monday – Friday: 9am -5pm

Aiobhneas (Joy)
Crisis Support
24-hr Freephone 1800 767 767
helpline@aoibhneas.org
WhatsApp - 0864136979
(deaf or hard of hearing)

Kildare
Teach Tearmainn (House of Asylum)
045-527584
helpline@teachtearmainn.ie

Kilkenny
Amber Refuge
Acorn
Lacken House
Dublin Road
Leggetsrath West
Kilkenny
R95 NY04
(056) 777 1404

Laois
Laois Domestic Abuse Service
https://www.laoisdomesticabuseservice.ie/
057 86 71100
lina@laoisdomesticabuseservice.ie
Kylekiproe
Portlaoise
Co. Laois
R32 KX8E

Longford
Longford Women's Link
Longford Women's Link CLG
Willow House
Ardnacassa Avenue
Longford
043 3341511
nfo@lwl.ie

Louth
Women's Aid Dundalk
info@womensaiddlk.net

Saint Monicas
Cambrickville
Avenue Road
Dundalk
Co. Louth
A91 F962

Meath
Meath Women's Refuge
24 hour confidential helpline
1800 46 46 46
support@dvservicesmeath.ie

Offaly
Offaly Domestic Violence Support Service
Tullamore
Cormac Street
Tullamore
Offaly
057 935 1886
info@odvss.ie

Westmeath
Esker House
Athlone Community Service Council CLG (ACSC)
Esker House Domestic Abuse Support Service
Dr Dobbs Memorial Home
Northgate Street
Athlone
Co Westmeath
Esker House: 0906 474122
24 Hour Crisis Helpline: 1800662288

Wexford
Wexford Womens' Refuge
24/7 Helpline 1800 220 444
https://wexfordwomensrefuge.ie/supports/
Wicklow
Anu Wicklow
9am-5pm, Mon-Fri
086 059 7560
Bray Women's Refuge
24 hrs a day, 7 days a week
01 286 6163

Connacht
Galway
Domestic Violence Response
1st Floor
Commerce House
Mountain Road
Moycullen
Co. Galway
H91 D9HD
091 866740

Leitrim
DVAS provides services in Sligo, Leitrim, and West Cavan.
Sligo Centre 071 91 41515

Mayo
Mayo Women's Support Service
Breaffy Road
Castlebar
Co. Mayo
F23 TK44
094 9025409
https://www.mwss.ie/outreach/

Roscommon
Roscommon Safe Link
Elphin Street
Boyle
Co. Roscommon
0719664200
info@roscommonsafelink.ie

Sligo
DVAS
071 91 41515
https://domesticviolence.ie/useful-contacts/
General supports
Sisi
Support for women who have experienced intimate abuse
https://sisi.ie/

Citizens Information
https://www.citizensinformation.ie/
0818 07 4000

Pieta House
www.pieta.ie
1800 247 247
Text 51444

Samaritans
https://www.samaritans.org/
116 123

Suicide or Survive
https://suicideorsurvive.ie/
01 272 2158

Turn 2 Me
www.turn2me.org
Text 50808

Spun Out
www.spunout.ie
Text 50808

HSE
https://www2.hse.ie/mental-health/services-support/supports-services/

Walk in my shoes
https://www.walkinmyshoes.ie/library/about-mental-health/gettinghelp

National Women's Council
https://www.nwci.ie/womens_mental_health_support

Safe Ireland
https://www.safeireland.ie/get-help/

Womens Aid
https://www.womensaid.ie/get-help/support-services/

HSE
https://www2.hse.ie/mental-health/life-situations-events/domestic-violence-and-abuse/

Always Here
https://www.alwayshere.ie/national-helplines/
Mens Aid
https://www.mensaid.ie/

Women4Women
https://women4women.ie/directory-of-services/minority-women/violence-against-women/

Migrants
https://nascireland.org/know-your-rights/domestic-abuse

Scotland
Womens Aid
Womensaid.scot
0131 226 6606
Scottish Womens Rights
www.scottishwomensrightscentre.org.uk

Wales
Welsh Women's Aid
www.welshwomensaid.org.uk

www.cardiffwomensaid.org.uk

England
Womens Aid England

Women's Aid: www.womensaid.org.uk
Refuge: www.refuge.org.uk/

USA
https://www.womenslaw.org/

USA Hotline Resources

Dating Abuse: 1-866-331-9474

National Domestic Abuse Hotline: The Hotline.org 1-800-799-7233

National Eating Disorders.org: 1-800-931-2237

Suicide Life Line: LinesforLife.org 1-800-273-8255 TALK (24/7/365)

Text 273TALK to 839863 (8am-11pm PST)

Alcohol and Drug Helpline:1-844-289-0879 (24/7/365)

National Child Abuse Hotline: 1-800-422-4453

National Center for Missing and Exploited Children: 1-800-THE-LOST (1800-843-5678)

National Sexual Assault Telephone Hotline: 1-800-656-HOPE (4673)

National Alliance on Mental Illness (NAMI) Helpline: 800-950-NAMI

National Mental Health Hotline: (866) 903-3787

American Association of Poison Control Centers: (800) 222-1222

America Social Health: STD Hotline: (800) 227-8922

Printed in France by Amazon
Brétigny-sur-Orge, FR